# SURVIVING HITLER

# SURVIVING HITLER

## THE UNLIKELY TRUE STORY OF
## AN SS SOLDIER AND A JEWISH WOMAN

## O. HÅKAN PALM

ᐱᐱ
®

DESERET
BOOK

Salt Lake City, Utah

**Library of Congress Cataloging-in-Publication Data**

Palm, O. Håkan, 1949– author.
    Surviving Hitler : the unlikely true story of an SS soldier and a Jewish woman / O. Håkan Palm.
        pages   cm
    Includes bibliographical references.
    ISBN 978-1-60907-847-8 (hardbound : alk. paper)
1.  Mormon converts—Sweden.  2. World War, 1939–1945—Personal narratives, Jewish.  3. World War, 1939–1945—Personal narratives, Norwegian.  I. Title.
    BX8693.P34 2014
    289.3092'2—dc23
    [B]                                                                                      2014005302

Printed in Canada
Friesens, Manitoba, Canada

10   9   8   7   6   5   4

To my parents
Gustav and Agnes Erdös Palm
and for their descendants
and all those whose lives
they have touched

# CONTENTS

# ACKNOWLEDGMENTS

I express my deep appreciation to the many individuals who have contributed to the creation of the book you now hold in your hands.

Lynn M. Hansen, who represented the United States in arms reduction talks with the Soviet Union, believed in this book from the beginning. In 2008, after hearing about my parents' story, he flew to Stockholm from Frankfurt to meet them. Two years later he offered to translate that story if I would write it. With his great wisdom, experience, and language skills, he became a kind mentor to me. In October 2013 we received with sadness the message that Lynn had suddenly passed away. He has my special thanks for his voluntary and masterful translation from Swedish to English. Together we worked hard, including fifteen-hour days for a full week doing check and control reading before our first meeting with Deseret Book. With humor, in front of others he called me his slavedriver!

Gösta Körlof, who is married to my sister Kristina, is a captain in the Swedish army reserves. He tirelessly researched military facts about the World War II battles in which my father served as a soldier on the front lines. He helped explain Papa's war experiences in their strategic context and importance. Through his research, Gösta could explain to Papa, for example, why he was driven by truck to various sectors of the front. Gösta also found facts about the battles for which Papa received awards for his heroic efforts.

Cory H. Maxwell, formerly director of publishing at Deseret Book and presently serving as a mission president, believed in the story fifteen years ago and engaged David Sandum to translate it. Professor Dean May was also involved, but unfortunately, the project stalled after his death. Cory was the one who in 2011 met with Lynn Hansen and me and then championed the idea at Deseret Book, which has resulted in the publication of this volume.

Lisa Roper, product director at Deseret Book, went not only the extra mile but also the third and fourth miles beyond that to suggest improvements to the manuscript and to prepare it for a publication decision. Heidi Taylor, also in product development at Deseret Book, envisioned the ideal format for the book and worked to restructure the manuscript into its present form. Without Heidi and Lisa, the book would not have reached you, the reader. It's a fact!

Other professional, experienced associates at Deseret Book have also made this book better. Especially I want to acknowledge an extraordinary editor, Suzanne Brady, typographer Malina Grigg, and designer Shauna Gibby.

President Thomas S. Monson, having much knowledge of World War II, understood the greatness of my parents' life stories and on several occasions urged me to write down their inspiring and unique life path to share with others.

Cristy Valentine, secretary to President Monson, has been involved in all the meetings my wife, Barbro, and I have had with President Monson over many years in Salt Lake City and in Sweden.

Barbro, my capable dear wife and mother to our seven children, worked behind the scenes with her knowledge of research and literature. Always with great patience, she has been my best counselor.

*President Thomas S. Monson visiting Gustav and Agnes Erdös Palm in their home in Haninge, Sweden, 2005.*

# INTRODUCTION

In 1995, something very special happened, which was a type of benediction on my parents' lives and especially my father's life. President Thomas S. Monson, then First Counselor in the First Presidency of The Church of Jesus Christ of Latter-day Saints, was assigned to divide the Sweden Stockholm Stake. The Mormon Church had grown significantly in Stockholm. Several times during the 1960s, 70s, 80s, and 90s, Elder (later President) Monson had visited in Stockholm. I had responsibilities that made it natural for me to meet with him during his visits to Sweden. At one of those visits in 1984, Elder Monson met my parents, Agnes and Gustav, for the first time, and he learned their life stories. As I interpreted for them, Elder Monson recorded everything in his memory.

Eleven years later, when he arose to speak at the end of the meeting, when all formalities for dividing the Stockholm stake had been completed, President Monson said, "This has been a real 'Palm Sunday.' Brother Gustav Palm's son-in-law Gösta has been chosen as the president of the new stake. Gustav himself has been given sealing power in the temple. And Gustav's son Håkan has been called to be in the leadership of the second stake."

Then, from memory, President Monson gave a very detailed account of my parents' lives. He said he felt the Lord had preserved

Agnes and Gustav through the war until they met: my mother as a Jewish Holocaust victim and my father as a voluntary Waffen-SS soldier.

This was the first time my father's history, including his enlistment in the Waffen-SS, was made public. From where I was sitting on the stand in front of 1,500 attendees, I could observe his facial expressions during the few minutes when his life's secret was revealed. He sat completely still, and it was difficult to determine what might have been going on in his mind. His knuckles whitened as his hands gripped the armrests of his chair.

Of course, all who knew my father regarded him with respect and admiration for the humble and devoted servant of the Lord that he was, and they continued to do so. I have never heard a single negative comment or sneer relating to my father's having fought in a German uniform during World War II. So, although he might have been embarrassed by the unexpected revelation in front of so many people, my father instead accepted the fact that an Apostle of the Lord was speaking of the reality of his life. Thus, a new gate was opened for him in the process of becoming reconciled to his past. He didn't have to hide much of himself any longer.

As a Holocaust victim, my mother experienced different postwar challenges. For her, the concentration camp experiences were nothing to be ashamed of, though they did have lasting repercussions.

Here, then, in their own words, is the story of my parents, Agnes and Gustav Palm.

# BEFORE THE WAR, 1919–1939

## Agnes

**1919, Tápiogyörgye, Hungary**

My name is Agnes Veronika Erdös Palm. I was born into a Jewish family on May 19, 1919, in Tápiogyörgye, Hungary, about sixty miles east of Budapest, where I lived until I was about six years old. My father was Oszkar Erdös, and my mother was Aranka Biliz. I was their only child. Because my father was employed as an overseer on estates owned by members of the aristocracy and later as the director of a big luxury hotel, I grew up as a child of privilege. ⚬

*Agnes and her mother, Aranka, in newly tailored winter clothes, 1930.*

3

## *Gustav*

### 1922, Spydeberg, Norway

I was born on October 24, 1922, in Spydeberg, in the part of Norway called Östfold. My father was Emanuel Palm, born in 1896, and my mother was Maria Haugland, born in 1879 and thus some seventeen years his senior. Because my father was a Swedish citizen,

*Maria at her home in Haugland, Norway, where she lived with her first husband and their seven children.*

I too was a Swedish citizen, even though we lived in Norway my first seven years. There our farm's name was Haugland. It was a small farm, about twenty-five miles south of Oslo.

In 1918, before I was born, my mother had lost her first husband, a man named Hans Thorgrimsen, to the Spanish influenza. It was a deadly pandemic that spread across much of the world. My mother had seven children with Mr. Thorgrimsen before he died. One day after my mother was widowed, Emanuel Palm happened by and was hired to help with the farmwork. Maria and Emanuel married in 1920 and had three children together, one of those children being me. My younger siblings were Erling and Thea. ❖

## *Agnes*

### 1923, Tápiogyörgye, Hungary

I remember my first feelings of happiness on a sunny and warm summer day in Tápiogyörgye. My mother was carrying me on her back and singing children's songs to me, her four-year-old daughter. We went through a small cluster of woods and into our vegetable garden in front of the house where we lived. Suddenly Mother stopped in the middle of the path. She set me down carefully and showed me a creature previously unknown to me. Lovingly, she told me that it was a snail that carried his house on his back and that snails crawl very slowly. Nearby, above the rippling brook, I spied large, shining green dragonflies darting among the reeds in the calmer water, and I could hear birds chirping in the hazelnut trees nearby. Once we reached the vegetable garden, my mother picked young peas and then we walked through the woods together on our very long way home to the manor.

Snails, dragonflies, birds singing, and my mother being happy—these things form my first conscious memory. It is a memory full of happiness. I remember the summer heat, my mother's strong arms a refuge, and her unconditional love for me, her only child. These form the foundation upon which I have built my confidence to face challenges and to be guided by internal principles rather than the opinions of others. ⇒⇐

## Agnes

**1924, Tápiógyörgye, Hungary**

In 1924, I turned five years old and experienced an ordeal that etched itself in my consciousness. For the first time I experienced pain, suffering, death, and the loss of a close friend. Although I was only five, I believe that this event laid the groundwork for my religious beliefs.

It was a clear September day with the sun standing high in the sky. I had two playmates. The girl's name was Mancia. She was two years older than I. The boy was not more than three years old. His name was Frans, but I called him Fetyo. That morning I sat on the porch steps of my home and waited for Mancia and Fetyo to come.

Instead, Fetyo's mother came running with tears and loud screams. She was completely out of breath. In her arms, she held a bundle. When she came closer, I saw two small, purple, swollen legs protruding from the bundle. Mother, the cook, the kitchen maid, and the nanny came storming out of the house. Terrified, we all looked at the small child in the blanket bundle. My mother yelled for the driver to get to the hospital in town as fast as possible. The driver hitched the fastest Lipizzaner horses to the best carriage and took off with the horror-stricken mother and the quiet child wrapped in blankets.

The little boy in the blanket was Fetyo. That morning he had been playing in the kitchen with a corncob while his mother fed the chickens. Suddenly a glowing ember popped out of the fireplace and set fire to the dry leaves around the corncob. Fetyo's clothes caught fire. His sister screamed, and their mother came running into the kitchen. There stood Fetyo, wrapped in flames from his burning clothes. His mother snatched a blanket, put out the fire, wrapped the child, and ran to our manor. The two small legs sticking out from the blanket were the last I saw of my beloved curly-headed playmate. The Lipizzaner horses ran as fast as they could but did not reach the doctor in time. My little friend died from the burns caused by the flames that had engulfed his body.

When my mother came home crying that afternoon, I asked where Fetyo was. She told me he was with God in heaven. Fetyo was now a little happy angel. After that, I often played and chatted with my little angel friend from heaven. For me, Fetyo was alive, and I sang for him. ⊰⊱

## Agnes
**1925, Alsóbesnyö, Hungary**

My father, Oszkar, accepted a job as a foreman for a count who owned large estates in Hungary and Austria. We moved to one of the count's vast estates in Alsóbesnyö, in the region of Fejér, a little more than forty miles south of Budapest. From there, Father led the work and supervised activities on the count's estates in both countries.

*Oszkar preparing to inspect the fields of the vast estate in Alsóbesnyö, Hungary.*

We lived a privileged life on a magnificent estate. I was pampered by the servants who told me many stories, mostly folk tales, and brought me joy. At school, I was given special status as the foreman's daughter, and the other children showed great respect to me, even though I was the youngest and smallest.

Every autumn we received a visitor: an old Romany, or Gypsy, woman. No one, not even she, knew how old she was. Her husband, children, and grandchildren lived in four covered wagons in which they wandered all over central Europe. The Gypsy woman and her family came to us every year and stayed a week in their wagons on the other side of the duck pond. She would sit at the entrance to our house with four large bags and wait. When she saw Mother, she greeted her with the salutation "Gracious lady" and then said that God had given her another year to live.

This was the signal for Mother and our cook to take the Gypsy woman's four empty bags and then go around and collect all the knives, scissors, and broken pots and pans on the estate to be mended and sharpened. Meanwhile, I sat on the stairs and chatted with the old Gypsy.

Her arms were covered in gold chains, and several gold necklaces adorned her neck. Some necklaces were made of silver coins. Her face was furrowed and beautiful. Around her waist were also chains that held up her long, colorful, embroidered skirts. The Gypsy woman belonged to another world, and I felt invited into it by her warmth and capacity to really see me. She told me about newborn babies and the intrigues of love. With big eyes, I listened and allowed myself to be fascinated.

Mother and the cook filled other canvas bags with advance payment in the form of flour, dried beans, smoked sausage, ham, and pork. The Gypsy woman could not carry all the bags of food and the bags of knives, scissors, and pans. She took the bags of food and said she would send one of her sons to retrieve the "work bags." I begged Mother to let me go with her to the Gypsy camp to see the newborn baby that the old woman had spoken of. Mother agreed, as long as my nanny went with me.

What an experience it was. The wagons were parked side by side in a semicircle, with the horses grazing in front of the wagons. I felt peace, curiosity, and a strange yearning. Everyone had his or her responsibilities, and their society enveloped me. The men sat on the ground around fires and sharpened knives or repaired pans. The boys obtained the dull knives from families in the countryside and returned them freshly sharpened. The girls followed the boys and returned with fabric and money. The women cooked over open fires and washed clothes in large wooden tubs. The little children played and romped like children do everywhere. Everyone in the camp honored the old Gypsy woman as if she were the queen. All activity ceased and the buzzing stopped when she walked into camp. All eyes were on us. I put my hand in the Gypsy woman's, and we went to a special wagon. On it sat a beautiful young woman. She nursed a newborn child that was wrapped in colorful quilts. I could see only the baby's curly black hair. The Gypsy woman lifted the baby down to me.

The little baby lay in my arms, and I was transported to a fairy-tale world. Never had I seen anything so beautiful and sweet. The little girl had a reddish-brown complexion, black eyes, and black hair. Jealousy took possession of me. Why didn't I have a little brother or sister? I yearned for that so much it hurt.

After about half an hour, my nanny took me by the hand and we waved and backed out of the camp. We took the dark way home to my clean and bare riches. For several days I was depressed, but I did not dare tell my mother that I yearned for the Gypsy camp and its happy family life. We were rich and had all the amenities. The gypsies were poor and had only their happiness. My feelings were much affected, but I did not understand how or why. I think my desire to be part of a large family with many children was born in the Gypsy camp just over half a mile from my own room.

That year, 1925, was also the year that my mother and father and I were baptized into the Catholic Church. It happened a few weeks before I started school. Mother, Father, and I went to the neighboring village of Nyarad in Veszprem county. After the morning service, all three of us were baptized into the Catholic Church. I remember that everyone else

*At age nine Agnes was confirmed in the Catholic Church, 1928.*

had gone home; only the priest, our godparents, and we remained. The priest pronounced some Latin phrases, sprinkled water on our heads using a small scoop, and swung his censer. After the baptism, Father said that we belonged to the Catholic Church, and if someone were to ask me my religion, I should reply that I was Catholic. ⇥⇤

## *Gustav*
### 1927, Spydeberg, Norway

When I was but five years old, I listened to a story exchanged between my father and a neighbor. It stuck in my memory and influenced my attitudes. It was a tragic story set in 1809, more than a century before.

At that time England had blockaded the coast of Norway and all the ports. There was a severe shortage of food throughout the country. One Norwegian man was obliged to obtain grain for seed and food for his family. If he was not successful, the whole family would starve. I listened with big ears to Father and the neighbor, who sat on the sofa and talked.

The man in my father's story heard that there was grain to buy in Denmark, but that was a long way off, and the English were vigilant in maintaining the blockade. The man felt he had no choice but to try to sneak past the lines of security. With his lightest boat, he reached Denmark, where he purchased three bags of barley and started back for Norway.

Along the coast there was thick fog, and as the sun burnt through, he saw to his horror that he was next to a British patrol boat. A sailor on the deck peered down at the Norwegian's boat, and then he raised his oar and ran it through the little row boat's bottom. The three sacks of grain fell through the hole, the boat sank, and the man was taken into custody. He prayed on his knees for mercy for himself and his family, but to no avail—he was taken prisoner to England. Five years later, he was released from his captivity and was returned to Norway. He searched for his family, but his wife and children had starved to death.

Though we never talked politics in our home, that conversation affected me so that I always thought of the English as threatening strangers. I had no friends with whom to discuss such things or from whom to gain any other perspective. There was simply no one to talk to. What I didn't know at the time was that the account of the Norwegian fisherman was fictional—that my father and his friend were discussing the plot of a poem written by Henrik Ibsen entitled "Terje Vigen," not an event that had happened in real life. In any case, this story would affect the way I saw the world. ⊰⊱

## Agnes
**1930, Papa, Hungary**

In the summer of 1930, I contracted measles. I had a high fever, and many days of bed rest were necessary. The village doctor visited several times. When a large abscess formed on my neck, the doctor operated on it without an anesthetic while I sat on the bed; I remember screaming out in pain. It resulted in a scar on my neck that has been visible throughout my life.

A few weeks later, I contracted whooping cough. Coughing attacks occurred around the clock, and I got weaker and more tired each day. Father and Mother decided that my teacher and I would travel up to Bakony Mountain for therapy. Once there, we lived in a small inn not far from the medieval cathedral with its monastery. In the monastery was a small and exciting library. My teacher and I often sat there and read books. The church and the monastery were filled with art treasures, and I was fascinated as I looked at them. My teacher's tales fueled my imagination. The pure, high

*Agnes (right) and her German-speaking private teacher.*

forest air helped a lot. After a week, I was almost fully healed, and we went home again.

I was able to spend two or three weeks of my summer vacation with my grandmother, who lived in my father's native town, Keszthely, at Lake Balaton. She was the last real daughter of Israel in our family. She was Jewish and lived piously according to the Torah.

I remember one evening when I lay next to my grandmother in her soft and deep sagging bed in her large bedroom. At that time, she spoke softly to me that she was glad she would soon rest in hallowed ground instead of experiencing the great tribulations that would soon come. Terrified, I listened as she said that her descendants would be persecuted to death. But, she said, God would protect me in spite of my experiencing such frightful things. Prophecies of the Jews' dispersion, suffering, death, and Israel's final vindication by a coming Messiah would be fulfilled, my grandmother said.

I never forgot my grandmother's words. ⇒⇐

# Gustav

## 1931, Väse, Värmland, Sweden

In 1929 my mother and father had bought a farm in Väse, Värmland, Sweden. On our farm two streams flowed together, and

*Gustav and his family at their farm in Väse, Sweden. Back, from left: half sister Margit; mother, Maria; and father, Emanuel. Front: Gustav; sister, Thea; and brother, Erling.*

my brother, Erling, and I fished there often. The creek was teeming with pike and bleak, so we helped provide food for our family.

When my sister, Thea, was two years old, Erling and I often took responsibility for her during the days, even when we went fishing. One day, we placed Thea on a tuft in the water where the two streams met. We felt sure she would not run away, but while we were busy, Thea fell into the water. At first we did not notice that she was gone, but Erling caught sight of Thea as she lay on the bottom of the creek. He quickly jumped in and managed to save our sister.

Of course, our mother became very upset when we returned home. Erling was disappointed that Thea stole all the attention and no one saw how he bled from the wounds he had received when he struggled to get Thea up to the air. He was certainly the neglected hero.

Often Erling and I teased Thea until she started to cry. Her tears made me quickly stop teasing and start to comfort her. Thea, therefore, learned to cry at once whenever we started to tease her. She knew I couldn't help feeling sorry for her. Often I took her on short walks and explained the world to her. I think she felt I was a kind big brother. ⇥⇤

## Agnes
**1931, Papa, Hungary**

My friends from the village worked from 6:00 in the morning to 6:00 in the evening with a two-hour lunch and siesta break at midday. That was ten hours of hard and tough toil every day, weeding beets in the large fields. Every Saturday at lunchtime, all the working children and other day laborers would stand in a long queue at the estate office to receive their wages, which for the children was two Hungarian pengö per day. One pengö was roughly equal to 20 cents in the early 1930s.

One Monday, after I had begged Father for a long time, he allowed me to go with my friends out to the fields like a real worker. By the lunch break, my strength was waning. The other children continued working at the same pace, but my hands and back ached more and more. When it was finally lunchtime, I sat down in the grass, relieved. The girl from our kitchen came with my lunch basket, and I shared hot dogs and drinks with the others. After lunch, we rested until 2:00 in the tall, cool grass, in ditches, or under apple trees planted in big boxes. Then we continued our work, and I had to push myself hard to keep up with my friends, who were more skilled and stronger than I was.

After my first twelve-hour day, I ached over my whole body

from working muscles I didn't ordinarily use. I did not eat any food when I got home but crept straight into my bed and fell asleep. Before that, however, I asked my mother to wake me up at a half-past five the next morning. The work went better the second day, and everyone was kind to me. Before bedtime I again asked Mother to wake me up the following morning, but Mother didn't have the heart to wake me, so I slept till well past eleven. Disappointed, I complained, but my days as a day worker were over. This period in my life concluded when I stood in the pay queue and received my first salary of four pengö for two long days of honest work.

With four pengö in my purse, I went with my mother the following week to Sopron to visit Grandma and Grandpa. Early on the day after we arrived, I took my four pengö to the toy store at the city bazaar. It gave me great joy to buy a toy with money I had earned myself. ⇒⇐

## Gustav
### 1934, Väse, Värmland, Sweden

During the summer my cousin Helge Palm from Långshyttan came to stay with us a couple of months. I liked him very much, and we worked together on the farm. Helge loved to fish in the creek on our farm just as much as I did. We enjoyed being together. Little did I know that he would play a significant role in my life eleven years later. ⇒⇐

*Cousin Helge Palm and Gustav fishing on the farm in Väse.*

## Gustav

### 1935, Grums, Värmland

My parents purchased a larger farm in 1935, and we moved to Grums, Värmland, Sweden. Father often went away to work in the forest and on other farms, and my brother, Erling, and I did the hard jobs on our farm and also took daytime jobs in the neighborhood. Our mother worked hard to get enough food on our table and money for other expenses.

*Erling and Gustav arriving at the farm in Haugland, Norway, after biking from their new home in Sweden.*

The distance to our half siblings in Norway was seventy-five miles, and Erling and I enjoyed biking there a few times.

One day when I was thirteen, my mother had a surprise for me. She and I went to an iron and chemicals business where we bought tools, nails, and screws for the farm. When we were finished, she asked if I would like to have some brushes and oil paints. "Of course," I answered, more than a little baffled.

Being supplied with equipment with which to paint, it was my task to choose the motif. I could not form humans and animals, but straight and simple lines worked. So I painted churches, although other buildings were certainly easier to paint. Did these motifs reveal something about the essence of my being? After a few church paintings, I got tired and put my paint brushes away. I never became adept at painting, but possibly the art helped to reveal part of my psyche.

My mother took over my brushes and oil paints; she had both the talent and the ability to express things artistically. However, her creative self-confidence had been curbed by difficult years of poverty, and she had not taken the initiative to start painting. She hoped instead that some of her children might have inherited her talents.

*Gustav's mother, Maria, in old age, after she moved back to Haugland, Norway. She is spinning yarn from wool fleece, and one of her paintings hangs on the wall.*

My parents divorced, and in 1939 Mother sold the farm in Sweden and bought a smaller farm in Onsöy, outside Fredrikstad, in Norway. There we grew fruit and vegetables and produced eggs. During harvest season, my sister, Thea, biked once a week to grocery shops in town and delivered the products. ✦

# *Gustav*

## 1939, Onsöy, Norway

My youthful experiences in Onsöy near the Oslo fjord were figuratively constrained by the limits of the islands in the fjord. It was tranquil without much outside interference. Nonetheless, there was an opening between the islands on the horizon. Many times I let my imagination wander and wondered what was out there in the world. Life seemed full of undiscovered potential, and I prepared myself to go out on a journey of discovery.

I was in my teenage years. One January day, the wind began to howl and propel itself along the ridges and bare mountainsides. Grains of snow swept across the surface of the fjord, first in one direction and then in the other. But my brother, Erling, and I were young, fit, and healthy, and as we rowed our boat against the wind down through the fjord, we experienced the uniqueness of the situation with a wonderful sense of awe. For weeks we had felled trees along the side of a valley. Finally, only a few trees remained at the top of the ridge, and we expected to complete our work during the short days in January.

We pulled our boat onto the shore, removed our backpacks, and began to fell and trim trees. The intensity of the work caused us to become soaked in sweat. The mercury stayed around ten degrees below zero Fahrenheit all day. The cold air froze the sweat into a frostlike coating on our clothes. Snow fell from the trees above us as we cut marks in the trunks to be cut down.

At noon we ate lunch. There was no shelter, so we each sat on our own snow-covered log and took out our sack lunches and thermoses. We ate our sandwiches, which contained thick slices of sour pickles. To some that might have seemed a luxury, but Mother, who had prepared the sandwiches, knew what we liked, and I remember her saying, "They are so young, and they work so hard.

They need all the food they take in." The meal did not last very long. Within minutes, the open-faced sandwiches were frozen by the icy wind, and we needed to get back to work to increase our body temperature.

Life taught us early what it took to be a man, but it also gave us the satisfaction of overcoming difficulties and knowing success. A good warm home, a crackling fire in the stove, and cooked food in the evening made us forget the challenges of the day. Our home was simple, but it was a priceless treasure to be there. The beginning of my adult life could have continued in all simplicity, free and enchanting. But I saw the future before me as including alluring adventures waiting to be experienced.  ❊❊

# YEARS OF WAR, 1939–1944

## Agnes
### 1939, Galyatetö, Hungary

In August 1939 we heard the radio broadcast reporting that Hitler had invaded Poland. At that time, Father and Mother were advisors to a government hotel project in the village of Galyatetö in the Carpathian Mountains, about sixty miles northeast of Budapest. There, the state had built a luxury hotel for wealthy people suffering from cardiovascular and lung disease. The hotel was constructed according to the highest international standard and decorated in the most modern style. My father had been hired as purchasing agent and Mother as human resources manager. The hotel was both a skier's paradise and a private sanatorium.

*The luxury hotel in Galyatetö where Agnes lived a comfortable life with her parents.*

For the two and a half years until the Nazi injunctions against the Jews, we lived a continued life of luxury and had many, many meetings with interesting people who were hotel guests, including the famous Hungarian composer Bela Bartok. Every afternoon we had tea at 5:00 with dancing in the bar. There I met my skiing and other hotel friends. At least two or three times a week, I was involved in activities in the bar. I drank chocolate with whipped cream and ate cake. Sometimes I danced a few turns.

*Agnes enjoyed skiing in the mountains near the hotel in Galyatetö.*

In the basement of the hotel was a tourist dining room that was a bit less expensive and decorated in rustic style; the canteen was also there. I ate in both dining rooms, alternating between them. They had lovely, hearty Hungarian fare.

Next to the administration office, we had our private dining room, where Mother, Father, and I could eat alone.

In the hotel in Galyatetö, I lived a real life of luxury.

---

*Starting in 1938, Hungary instituted a series of anti-Jewish measures. The laws defined a person as a Jew if he or she had one Jewish grandparent, and Jews' participation in society was restricted politically and economically (Friedländer 1, 236; 2, 266).*

---

## Gustav

### 1939, Onsöy, Norway

My brother, Erling, and I were preparing a field that we had recently claimed from the forests. We had carried away the last roots and hauled away the last big rocks and were preparing the earth where we intended to plant potatoes in the spring. Suddenly we saw Mother running toward us. Full of excitement and with tears choking her voice, she shouted that war had broken out between England and Germany. Erling and I felt that these countries were so far away—why should their war affect us? If they wanted to fight each other, it was none of our concern. On the other hand, Mother was probably thinking of rationing, suffering, and deprivation along with possible physical injury and violent death.

We continued with our main job of preparing the soil for planting. The feeling of having accomplished something important filled us. We could not fully understand what war between England and Germany might mean to us. Our potato field was more immediate and understandable.

The people in our neighborhood were upset by the radio news and newspaper articles, and the news had all their attention. Everywhere it was discussed passionately and recklessly; some were for one country and others for the other. Even though the war began to touch more and more countries, we still believed it was a war primarily between England and Germany. ❊❊

> *On August 23, 1939, Nazi Germany and Communist Soviet Union signed a nonaggression agreement, including a secret provision dividing eastern Europe into two spheres of interest between Germany and the Soviet Union. The agreement was called the Molotov-Ribbentrop Pact.*
>
> *Only a week later, on September 1, 1939, Germany attacked Poland. France and Great Britain responded quickly and declared war with Germany within a few days. World War II had begun.*
>
> *The Soviet Union invaded eastern Poland on September 17, 1939, and six weeks later, on November 30, 1939, attacked*

*Finland. Both Poland and Finland had previously been part of the Russian empire before World War I but had become independent states after that war. It appeared that Josef Stalin wanted to include all former Russian territory in the Soviet Union.*

*The nonaggression pact held until June 22, 1941, when Germany attacked the Soviet Union, and the two countries were at war. Russia then became allied with France and Great Britain* (Nationalencyklopedin, *14, 197, 283, 306, 343, 350, 375–76*).

## Gustav

1940, Onsöy, Norway

On April 9, 1940, when Mother heard that Germany had invaded Norway, she ran to a neighboring farm to call her seven other children. Overwhelmed by everything that was happening, she returned home to tell us that her sons at Haugland had reported to the nearest military installation and that their cousins had done the same. All the men of an appropriate age had gone to pick up military equipment.

Little by little, we learned about the inadequacies of the Norwegian defense and how the Germans easily occupied one city after another. The king and leaders of the Norwegian government fled the country.

*On April 9, 1940, Germany attacked Denmark and Norway. Germany occupied Norway by June 10, 1940, when the last battle with regular units ended. The Soviet Union occupied the Baltic countries of Estonia, Latvia, and Lithuania in the summer of 1940 (Friedländer 1,167; 2, 266).*

A lot happened in a very short time, and everything seemed to be turned upside down. Norway was without a king or government,

*German soldiers march through Oslo, Norway.*

and the German victory was complete. An intense propaganda campaign began. People believed anything they heard. The Norwegian people separated into two camps—one friendly to the Germans and the other, the predominant one, in favor of the British. Between them was a merciless war of words. Common sense did not exist. A freeze on prices was instituted and a ban on strikes issued. We had to give part of our small hay harvest to the state.

Everyone began talking about a person of whom I had never heard: Vidkun Quisling. He was a Norwegian politician who seized power in a Nazi-backed coup that garnered him international infamy. His name would become synonymous with traitor. But at that point, I had the impression that he was someone in whom we could trust.

In the autumn of 1940, the German high commissioner in Norway was the Nazi Josef Terboven. In a speech to the Norwegian people, he promised full freedom and independence for the

Norwegian people who rallied around the political party *Nasjonal Samling,* or National Socialist Party (NSP).

What was I to do? If we obeyed the demands of the high commissioner, then it seemed to me that we had not committed a treasonous act. If we went against the Germans, would it be possible that we could hope for freedom again in the foreseeable future? But what about treasonous thoughts? The country's army had been routed, the king had abandoned the country in defeat, and the government had fled to another country. Could such a government be said to represent Norway? And what were England's intentions when it mined Norwegian waters and made efforts to take control of Norway's railways? On the other hand, did we have any guarantee that freedom would be restored if we went along with Terboven's proposition?

Such thoughts tumbled around in my young mind. No one was willing or able to give me guidance. One year after Josef Terboven's famous speech, I decided to join the National Socialist Party, and I became a member in January 1942. When my family and neighbors found out what I had done, it was a huge shock to them. Nevertheless, even then no one gave me any counsel on what I should or should not do.

When I came in contact with the National Socialist Party, I met people with independent ideas, enterprising and bold, and I shared many of those ideas. The people were ambitious and fully engaged, believing deeply in what they were being taught. But there were also others among them, most noticeable because of their unsavory behavior. ❥

# Agnes

## 1941–44, Keszthely, Hungary

Agnes before a traditional masquerade in Keszthely.

Things began to change in 1941 for my family and me. Hitler's influence increased throughout the continent of Europe. Laws discriminating against Jews were created right and left. Due to the new anti-Jewish laws, despite our baptism into the Catholic Church, my parents lost their jobs at the luxury hotel. We left Galyatetö and bought a vineyard just outside Keszthely, near the beautiful Lake Balathon. There we hoped to live a calm family life. Father experimented with different grapes and got good harvests. For almost three years we lived close to many of our extended family. Often we visited relatives after church on Sundays, and we cousins met at the Balaton beach and participated in balls. I sang in the Catholic choir, practiced piano, and loved to visit my older relatives.

For three years I studied Hungarian folk music and taught myself to play more than three hundred folk melodies on the piano. My piano teacher and I played Gypsy music, and we sounded like a complete Gypsy orchestra. The son of my piano teacher actually played every week in a Gypsy orchestra whose music was broadcast by the national radio station in Budapest. He worked in the foreign ministry and was married to a noble girl. On his holidays he visited his mother in Keszthely and gave me piano lessons in Gypsy music. He was so pleased with me that he wanted to play duets with me on the radio. His proposal was approved by the radio management. I would play the melody and he would accompany me in piano set parallel to mine.

The decision for us to play was made in Budapest in 1943, and we were scheduled to play together in April 1944. But in between came Hitler's occupation of Hungary on March 15, which stopped any plans for my role in a debut piano exhibition. ⇒⇐

> The Hungarian anti-Jewish laws of 1941 were similar to the German Nuremberg Laws of 1935 in taking away the civil rights of Jews, including the right to vote. Jews employed by the state were forced to leave their jobs (Friedländer 2, 226, 265).

## Gustav

Early 1942, Onsöy, Norway

In the beginning of 1942, I was a passive member of the National Socialist Party and attended just a few political meetings. One day, I received a letter with a form, which was already completed in full. My signature was the only thing missing. I could place a checkmark to indicate whether I chose military service for any period from half a year up to four years. The Norwegian battalion had been established.

I was not inclined to any of the options and was not at all in favor of a life in the military. As the oldest son in the family, I instead continued to support the family by working on our small farm in Onsöy and doing part-time jobs around the area.

A large party meeting was held in Vestfold on the west side of Oslofjord, and the highlight was Prime Minister Josef Terboven's visit and speech. All NSP members were required to attend. With members from many different places, the meeting was to be a major manifestation of the Party's popularity.

Together with 150 others, I stayed overnight in the gym at a school during the party meeting. We slept on the hard floor. Twelve men were taken out to be guards. Unfortunately, I was one of those chosen and had to be up part of the night.

During the night, the rain trickled down, and we guards walked through the wetness and watched over the camp's security. The cold rain was hard on idealism! We who had night duty were exempt from the marches and activities of the following day. The camp ended with a sports festival in the Horten stadium.

During 1942, an officer from the Hirden group asked me if I was interested in a good job. He then gave a long discourse about my duty to the Party and the country and that we must allow private interests to recede into the background. The work he offered, he said, had better prospects than farming could provide. The country needed police, and they would ideally be recruited from within the Party. "Police?" I repeated. "Regular traffic police here in the street?"

"Yes, right!" replied the sergeant.

Why not? I thought. I had plans to study at an agricultural college and had applied to a number of schools, but agricultural and forestry work were physically demanding. If they wanted me to join the police and they could place me in a situation that fit my requirements, I should consider it. After a little reflection, I decided that the offer was enticing. A police officer had a good income and secure employment. I took the leap and signed up for police training.

Before I heard back from the agricultural school, I received a letter from the police academy. It informed me that I was to report at the police barracks in Oslo for a medical examination. Then began the long nightmare of training. ⇒⇐

# Gustav

## Summer 1942, Oslo, Norway

Morale in the police academy was poor. Weeks before, we had been warned by others about the disagreeable training and encouraged to run away while we had the chance. Now we understood why. Regardless, it was hard to comprehend why a hard military course was added to my traffic police training.

No matter what the weather, every morning we exercised outdoors in special uniforms. After that, we would clean ourselves up, change into our regular uniforms, and make our beds. Then we would clean and dust the dormitories, the hall, and the stairs, clean the toilets, and finally eat breakfast.

Making the bed was a science. The sheet would have to be folded in specific ways to be absolutely flat on the mattress, folded under the pillow in a small crease, and remain at a 90-degree angle to the bed in front of the pillow. All that was very difficult because the mattress and the pillow were stuffed with lumpy wool. The lumpy wool caused us a lot of problems. It could not be smoothed out, and the constable was intransigent. If our beds were not properly made, he threw the bedding onto the barracks floor. Often the contents of our closets were also thrown into the mix because they were not suitably arranged. We had to work at a frantic pace to get things done before the beginning of the day's activities.

From 7:30 until noon, we underwent stringent training. It must have been a scourge for the entire city since all seventy-five of us were repeatedly ordered to scream at the top of our lungs. One of the staff taught us all the commands and then we had to memorize them to be able to shout them out.

Days became weeks. Our resistance was systematically broken down. We had to hear constantly how little we were worth, how miserable we were, how stupid we were, and how impossible it was to teach us anything. Our instructor summed up his attitude: "If I had ten real bullets, I would load the gun with them and shoot you. It's the only thing you are good for!"

Of course, we became frustrated; hatred and spite germinated within us against our officers. All actions taken in open opposition were punished with great attention. Finally, we just had to bow our heads and let our wills be subjugated. Now we just followed orders. All we did was carry out orders and directives. Everything was regulated in detail.

Finally we reached the level where the officers wanted us. We received the orders, and like machines we carried them out without thinking or looking for alternative approaches to executing the orders. We did just as we had been taught. All civilian thinking was gone.

At one point near the end of our training, the Norwegian captain gathered us and made a short speech. He said, "You may think that you are being mistreated, and perhaps you are thinking of fleeing to Sweden. That is no solution. During the last training period, two men tried that. They were captured at the border, and now they are sitting in the red house over there [he pointed to the prison], where they will sit for at least six months. I myself have sentenced them, and the same thing will happen to you if you try to escape." ⇒·⇐

## *Gustav*
### Autumn 1942, Tönsberg, Norway

In the autumn of 1942, my first assignment was not as a traffic policeman but as a guard at the newly opened camp named Berg, located just outside of Tönsberg, Norway. Everything seemed improvised, but now I realize that every little event must have been carefully orchestrated. To our great surprise, a transport of political

*The camp at Berg was one of the the worst prison camps in Norway.*

prisoners (in reality mostly Jews) was brought to the place where we were. A feeling of disquiet spread among us. In addition to us Norwegian guards were a few supervising German noncommissioned officers (NCOs). I realized later that we were quite literally prisoners guarding prisoners.

After three days, I could not deal with the situation anymore, so I went to the office and said I wanted to resign. I was told, however, that while I had been in training, a new law had been passed, which I understood to mean that a person could not resign from his position except in the case of an emergency. When I again asked to resign, the officer asked me if the living quarters were unsatisfactory, if the food I received was bad, or if my pay wasn't good. Of these matters I couldn't complain and said that what displeased me was my job—period. That, I was informed, was not an acceptable reason, and my request was ignored. Had I been sufficiently enterprising, I might have found a way to get away.

To maintain discipline in the camp, we used on the prisoners the same methods that had been used on us during our training. We ordered prisoners to flatten themselves on the ground and then stand up again. We had not learned any other way to deal with rowdy prisoners. Whenever I ordered a punishment, a biblical phrase would run through my head: "Roll in the dust." Like a bolt from the blue, I was gripped by an inexplicable sense of shame and would stop the punishment. It might seem as if those experiences were a small thing, but they were important to me. Why did I have feelings of shame? How was it that things had developed as they did? I pondered a great deal on what was happening within me.

The Germans who worked in the camp tried to incite us to shoot the prisoners. Certainly, they were joking! They wanted us to act tougher. We were constantly subjected to accusations that we were too lenient with the prisoners. Nonetheless, we managed in such a way that the Germans never took over the task of guarding the prisoners themselves. We never inflicted physical abuse on the prisoners, and none of them died during the time I was in the camp.

Our treatment of prisoners was not the best, but it was no worse than the treatment we ourselves had endured during our training. Perhaps it seemed much worse to the prisoners. We, as guards, were also prisoners, even though technically we had our freedom. None of us had voluntarily sought the task we were tricked into. These experiences might have seemed trivial, but for me they were important. ⇒⇐

## Gustav
### Mid-1943, Berg, outside Tönsberg, Norway

The Nazism I had been in contact with so far was not at all what I had imagined it to be. I had simply been very naïve. I was now fully convinced that the organization to which I belonged was wrong. I had developed a deep contempt for it. But now there was no return, and all I could do was to continue. My dilemma was that I had been misled about police training and I hated the task I had been given to be a camp guard at Berg. It was far from being the promised traffic police. To get away, I decided to volunteer as a Waffen-SS soldier to serve in the SS Schijägerbattalion Norwegen (SS Ski Ranger Battalion Norway), which was assigned to fight in Finland.

So, about half a year after I applied for leave, I received a short furlough and visited the recruiting office in Oslo. There, I filled out a form and submitted it to an NCO. For some reason I signed up for two years of service. The NCO changed the time to "for the duration of the war" with the justification that the war would not last two years. Finally, he gave me a note with the street address where I was to report and provided instructions on how to get there. I was told that I was a volunteer SS soldier (all Norwegian volunteers ended up in the Waffen-SS).

I was drawn to the idea of fighting for another Scandinavian country. That was the idealism of my youth. From November 30, 1939, to March 12, 1940, the Finns had fought the Winter War against the Soviet Union and then experienced the Continuation War, which began in June 1941. The Finnish struggle against the large, powerful Soviet empire was, I believed, a defense on behalf of the rest of Scandinavia. After all, what would happen if Finland were defeated? Wouldn't Sweden and then Norway be Russia's next objectives?

I believed I would be able to support Finland's cause against Communism but had to do so in the uniform of a Nazi Waffen-SS soldier. I had chosen which side I was to be on, and now I had to take the consequences of that choice and make the best of it.

The training of a Waffen-SS soldier included preparation at the fortress at Kongsvinger, Norway. On the schedule were lectures about national socialism and Darwinism, sports, and exercise, which consisted exclusively of the parade. We learned to present ourselves admirably in all aspects of the training. Chivalry, good posture, strength, power, boldness, and courage were held in high esteem. Our instructors were Norwegians and good role models.

After the course was completed, we all left for Oslo, where we were handed Norwegian rifles, divided into companies, and given Norwegian SS officer trainees as company officers. We regarded the civil population as our countrymen, not as enemies. They, however, regarded us as enemies. At that time, we did not know the role we played in German propaganda.

Within the German SS organization in Norway were held meetings, deployments, and the like. The atmosphere was lively, but it lacked leadership. Members attempted as best they could to accomplish the work. At one point, we were assigned to put up as many posters as we could. We were to do this at night so that when the people got up in the morning, the posters would greet them from every direction. A car and chauffeur were put at my disposal. We went over a large area and set up our posters. Many more of my colleagues were also in full action. Thousands of posters were put up.

But in the morning all the posters I had put up on my mile-long circular route had been torn up. The posters remained, but virtually all of them were ripped to shreds.

At the end of 1943, after the training in Norway was completed, I was transferred to Waffen-SS boot camp training in Hallein, Austria.  ⊱⊰

*Because Scandinavians are considered Germanic peoples, it was in line with Nazi ideology to recruit them. They were particularly sought after for military service in the Waffen-SS. The first unit formed, which included many Scandinavian volunteers with*

German officers, was the 5th SS Division Wiking. Its first deployment in battle was June 22, 1941, in Operation Barbarossa, the code name for Germany's invasion of the Soviet Union. About two years later, the Nordland regiment in the Wiking division, with approximately 2,100 volunteers from Scandinavia, became the basis for a new division, called the 11th SS Division, Nordland. Gustav Palm was assigned to Regiment Norway in that division. The officers were mainly German (see Tieke, 8, 10, 231).

## Agnes

**March 1944, Keszthely, Hungary**

On March 19, 1944, the Germans invaded our country. The weeks from then until the first of May were terrible. On that date, both those practicing the Jewish faith and those of Jewish descent, like us, were ordered to move into the ghetto—two old streets in the center of Keszthely. They had been cleared for our arrival. Although my parents and I had converted to the Catholic Church in the 1920s, the government considered us Jews.

After two weeks in the ghetto, all healthy persons between eighteen and fifty years of age were ordered to report to the town square. In military formation we marched from the square to the Festetics Palace to work on the estate of the grand duke. We were one hundred fifty to two hundred people who now became agricultural workers. I ended up with five other girls in the palace garden where we were to clean rosebeds. Though we were engaged in forced labor, our days were strangely pleasant and our life agreeable in the spacious, leafy castle garden. Nonetheless, we felt darkness far below the surface of our conversations.

Unaccustomed to manual labor, I quickly got blisters on my hands, and my back ached for the first few days. But the back pain disappeared as the days passed, and the blisters turned into hardened calluses. For me it was a special feeling when we were paid every Saturday afternoon. I was twenty-five years old, and this was my first job since the two days of labor in the beet fields during my childhood. After I was paid, it was a good feeling to give Mother the money I had earned. She too was in the ghetto, taking care of the household, and every penny was needed to help pay for food, the price of which escalated every day.

One Saturday when I picked up my wages, my best friend's father sat in the castle office as the paymaster. He was seventy years old and a notary. He had been brought in to replace the castle's accountant, who had received orders to report for military duty. As I stood in front of my friend's father, he quietly said to me that if I hid in the park when the others left for the ghetto, then he would come and get me after it was dark. I would then come with him and stay at his house, and they would hide me in their

*Keszthely is now an idyllic, picturesque town near Lake Balathon.*

small village. He had been informed
that in a few days the ghetto would be
emptied and that everyone was to be
transported to a concentration camp
in Poland. I asked if my parents could
come along. I thought that if we postponed the notary's plan by a few days,
they could accompany me to the castle
and then we could all three hide.

The answer I received was that
what I proposed was completely unthinkable. Crucial decisions had to be
made at once; moreover, the risk was
too great if the old notary were to hide
three people. The Germans had imposed very strict penalties for those

*Agnes and her mother, 1939.*

who hid Jews. I thanked him for his offer and replied that I could
not accept. My friend's father wept and hugged me. "You are a pre-
cious daughter and a good soul," he whispered. "May God bless
you, whatever may happen."

I could not imagine what my parents would do if I did not go
back to the ghetto that night. I went home in the evening as usual
and said nothing about the offer I had turned down.

The next morning the order came that no one was to leave the
ghetto, not even to go to work. For a terrible week we were not told
anything. We were sitting idle, brooding and foreboding. We dared
not put into words what we believed awaited us.

I was probably the only one who really knew.

On one of the mornings, when I was in the garden belonging
to the house where we lived in the ghetto, I heard someone whisper my name. In the bushes I recognized a man we knew as The
Painter, a man who sang tenor in our church choir. He had bribed

the guards at the entrance to the ghetto blockade. If I went with him, he explained, the guard would let us pass; he would then hide me with a relative who lived far out in the countryside. I replied that I had to take my mother and father. The Painter replied that was impossible and would put everyone in his family in jeopardy. I thanked him and for the second time turned down a rescue plan for me.

The Painter pressed my hand and said, "Whatever happens to you, I had to try and save you so my conscience would be clear. I could not look at myself in the mirror again if I did nothing for you here in the ghetto. We can only help one person, and you were the obvious one we wanted to save." We embraced each other and parted.

I thought within myself, "Honour thy father and thy mother: that thy days may be long upon the land which the Lord thy God giveth thee" (Exodus 20:12). Quiet peace descended on me, and fear disappeared. A perfect calm filled my soul. I felt that I had made the right choice. Oddly enough, this inner peace remained with me throughout most of the following year. ⇒⟨

> In April 1944, Hungarian authorities ordered half a million Jews living outside Budapest to move to ghettos and camps. Hungarian gendarmes were sent into the rural regions to round up the Jews and dispatch them to the cities (Friedländer 2, 652).

## Gustav
### Early 1944, Hallein, Austria

After a beautiful journey by train through Germany, I finally reported to the Waffen-SS boot camp and marched to equipment issue. All the instruction and drills were conducted in German. Our ability to understand was surprising, despite the fact that very few of us could speak German. For me, the training was repetitious; there was little that was new to me.

In the evening of the sixth day after arriving in Hallein, I had to find the dispensary. I was so sick that I could not wait to go there even though the time for medical visits was at 9:00 in the morning. I asked one of my comrades in the barracks, who was German, if he would accompany me to explain to the paramedics about my situation. Rather than go with me, he taught me that I should say, "Ich bin krank. Ich bin krank. Ich bin krank."

I stumbled to the sick barracks, where I said to a medic, "I . . . Isch is krank." At first I was yelled at because I had come at the wrong time, but a thermometer showed that I had a fever of 103°. I was put into one of the dormitories, and on his regular rounds the following day a doctor said that I had scarlet fever. A few hours later, I was in an ambulance with another Norwegian on the way to the hospital in Salzburg. Oh, how nice it was to be in a real bed and without the risk of being disturbed by shouting officers. The nurses treated me like a human being and tried as best they could to make me comfortable. Though I was sick, my time in the infirmary was glorious.

During his rounds next morning, the doctor examined me and said, "Oh, you are one unlucky bird. You also have diphtheria." He told the nurse to provide serum both for me and for the rest of the patients in the room. Afterward, I was moved to the diphtheria section in the hospital's main building. To my surprise, most of the sick were Norwegians.

Scarcely had I recovered from the scarlet fever and diphtheria than another throat disease had me in bed again. My body was so overextended that fever broke out. One afternoon, I was so bad that a special doctor was called in. My heart rate fell; I had shortness of breath and was not very alert.

The head doctor had been promoted, and a new one came in

his place. He was very ambitious and energetic, and his first action was to release as many patients as possible. He thought I could get adequate treatment in the camp, so I was hastily released and sent back to Hallein. At the boot camp, the officers found me too weak for training, and I was given a furlough. That gave me opportunity to take the train back to Norway and visit my family in Onsöy, outside Tönsberg, for a few weeks.

Because I was sick, I did not deploy with my unit when they were sent to Finland to fight the Russians. Later, I found out that my sickness was a blessing in disguise because everyone in that unit, save just a few, were killed. ⤞

## *Agnes*
### June 15, 1944, Keszthely, Hungary

At 7:00 in the morning they came to the ghetto. SS soldiers and interpreters went through each apartment. They explained that the SS at exactly that hour had taken over responsibility for us from the Hungarians. We were ordered to get ready for the march to the railway station in Keszthely. Because of what my friend's father had told me, I knew what others had only sensed concerning what awaited us.

Oddly enough, my whole being was still filled with a warm, calm, and comforting feeling.

I helped my mother and father to pack and then strolled around and joked with friends nearby. Many were despondent, others hysterical, and some shouted out their bitterness. For some reason, I, who had always been afraid and uncertain, now felt an inner strength and peace.

That Monday morning, Mother, Father, and I, together with five hundred others, marched through Keszthely. The streets were nearly empty except for the people in our march. At least a hundred SS soldiers with loaded rifles and fixed bayonets, along with barking German Shepherd dogs, kept us moving. Behind the closed windows of the buildings we passed, I saw both crying and laughing faces. One brave woman dared to open her third-floor window. She shouted, "Good-bye . . . the next time it will be our turn. May God . . ." Tears choked the rest of her words, and she shut the window.

We were led to a siding in the railyard. There stood a train with fifteen freight cars. The soldiers divided us so that we were approximately forty persons per car. The side door of our car was open. It was a long way up from the ground to the wooden floor of the freight car. Children, adolescents, couples, old men, and old women helped each other up into the crowded car. We sat on our bundles and suitcases. My father thought we were going to Germany, but others believed it would be Poland. We had listened to the secret and forbidden radio broadcasts from the BBC that told us about the concentration and extermination camps. For us, it had been impossible to believe in such inhuman cruelty and organized killing. We rationalized that the BBC's scare reporting was war propaganda. As the freight car door slammed, we dared not imagine what was ahead of us.

After a six-hour journey, the train stopped, and SS soldiers opened the door. I looked out and saw the sign: Zalaegerszeg. We were then in the county seat of Zala County, Hungary. Loudspeakers bellowed out that all of the county's three thousand Jews were to be interned in a large ghetto to await peace or to be exchanged for American or English prisoners of war. With innocence and faith we trusted what the loudspeaker said. We were appallingly deceived. And reality would far surpass the horror of our wildest fantasies and the BBC's prohibited descriptions of what for us was now becoming unthinkable reality.

We lined up alongside the train and were then herded like a

flock of sheep into a large, old, disused brickyard with a factory and a four-story warehouse. Both buildings were very rundown and located about five hundred yards apart. In front of the warehouse was a large enclosure filled with clay soil. It had probably been the raw material for the brick factory. Mother, Father, and I, together with our friends from the ghetto, climbed up to the fourth floor and further up into the attic. The sun shone from a blue sky, and it was terribly hot in the unventilated attic.

The oldest among us lay down indifferently on the floor. Those of us who were still functioning fetched pillows and blankets and handed them out to families. With sheets and string we tried as best we could to screen off our private family area. Farther away in the attic, three people chose to take their lives by hanging themselves or swallowing poison. Others tried to kill themselves by cutting themselves but failed. In other parts of the spacious attic, children were fighting and playing as if nothing had happened. Mothers wept or sat with vacant eyes that stared straight ahead out of despair. Most fathers were in military service at the front or in work camps. ❧❧

## Agnes
**June 1944, Zalaegerszeg, Hungary**

More than 90 percent of the physicians in Hungary were of Jewish descent. Among our group of about five hundred Jews from Keszthely were more than twenty physicians. Several of them were highly skilled specialists. In the storage building, they established a medical practice that was open virtually around the clock. The equipment was substandard, but the motivation of doctors and other personnel compensated for much of what was lacking.

My father was chosen to be the medical courier, which involved making a trip each morning in a German military Jeep to the hospital in Zalaegerszeg or pharmacies at other regional hospitals to obtain medicines for our field hospital. I was appointed to be Father's assistant and went with him every day as he made his rounds in the Jeep. We were the only ones allowed outside the barbed wire that surrounded the entire camp area. Of course, we were rigorously guarded by the driver and another guard in the SS Jeep.

During the final days in the park in Keszthely, I had gotten an infection in one thumb. It got worse day by day. A doctor in the field hospital had operated on it, but he did not have enough surgical supplies to completely cure the infection, which had started to attack the bone in my thumb. With sadness in his eyes, he told me he knew how to cure the infection but that he was unable to do more. The pain was almost unbearable. Nonetheless I was determined to go with Father in the SS Jeep again next morning.

At the regional hospital, after visiting the pharmacy, Father and I went immediately into the hospital itself. It was a risky side trip, which required courage and determination, especially on my father's part. Our guards were in the SS Jeep waiting for our return. We ran down a long corridor and knocked on a door with a sign indicating it was an operating room. A young, exhausted doctor asked who we were looking for and what we wanted. Father indicated I should show my thumb to the physician. "We have to deal with that immediately," he said. The infection had started to swell all the way up to my armpit. We had to hurry; the soldiers in the SS Jeep would be suspicious of a long visit to the pharmacy.

The doctor lanced my thumb without anesthesia. I think I fainted and hardly heard the doctor say, "I have saved the finger." Then he placed a large bandage on it. When the doctor found out where we had come from, he urged us not to tell anyone what he had done.

The pharmacist had now begun to look for us and no wonder,

for it appeared that we had escaped. If that had been the case, he could have been punished by death. When we showed up at the pharmacy, the pharmacist looked very relieved. He said nothing. Father and I took the drugs that had been placed on the counter. Together with the pharmacist, we hurried out to the Jeep. The soldiers grumbled a little and were upset that the trip to the pharmacy had taken so long. The pharmacist apologized to the soldiers but said nothing about my bandage, which I concealed as best I could. Or perhaps the pharmacist had not seen the bandage. We exhaled deeply, the pharmacist was relieved, and soldiers drove at a high speed back toward the camp. We arrived only thirty minutes later than normal, if one could speak of a normal arrival time.

Believing in God as Father and I did, we knew we were recipients of His inspiration and protection. But if one does not believe in God, then one would say it was pure luck and resourcefulness. Anyway, the infection had been cured, and I could use the thumb quite normally after a few days. ❧❧

## *Agnes*
**July 5, 1944, Zalaegerszeg, Hungary**

After three weeks in the old brick factory, we were ordered to prepare ourselves again to march to the side track at the railway station. We were up early in the morning and surrounded by soldiers who marched us in groups about two miles to a waiting freight train. We lifted and pulled each other up and got into our respective cars against the background noise of barking German Shepherd dogs and ear-piercing screams of the NCOs who were directing the activity.

The doors of the railcars slammed shut, one after the other. We were petrified with fear inside the car. Our despair was interrupted

A few weeks after the German army occupied Hungary, the deportation of the Jews began in May 1944 with mass transports to Auschwitz. The train that transported Agnes and her parents into Auschwitz on July 8, 1944, was one of the last trains of Hungarian Jews who were sent to Auschwitz from the countryside in Hungary. That transportation stopped July 9, 1944.

In 1941, Hungary had about 825,000 Jews, of whom 250,000 lived in Budapest. Of the Jews who lived in the countryside, 438,000 were sent to Auschwitz; 394,000 of them were killed upon arrival. The Jews of Budapest were deported in the fall of 1944. It was then that the Swedish diplomat Raoul Wallenberg showed great courage by intervening to rescue thousands of Budapest Jews, men, women, and children (Friedländer 2, 265, 657, 680).

occasionally by a hysterical scream or the noise of someone taking care of their needs in the toilet bucket. Such humiliation!

Numb, we fell asleep but were awakened by the train's monotonous motion and hard thumps. It must have been on the morning of July 6 when in a low voice my father said to me, "Sit up, my girl. Following Israel's old example and the traditions of our ancestors, I want to give you a patriarchal blessing." I was not surprised, even though we had been faithful Catholics for many years. All around us, older men were laying their hands on the heads of their family members, murmuring blessings in Hebrew. I

*A cattle car like those that transported Agnes, her parents, and other Jews to Auschwitz-Birkenau.*

*Oszkar Erdös, Agnes's father, as a young man.*

did not understand anything that they said.

My father laid his hands upon my head and in the Hungarian language put into words his patriarchal blessing. In the blessing, he said that Mother's life and his days of torment would soon be over. They would be killed and be with God; however, they would not suffer. Father continued his blessing and told me that in spite of much suffering, I would survive. I was young and of a pure heart. Father's spirit would protect me so that I would eventually find "the truth." He assured me that in the future we would be reunited with God and His Son Jesus Christ. For me it felt very natural that Father, who was a Catholic, should give me a Jewish blessing. I never wondered about the strangeness of this. My father said many other things, but I do not remember everything. I felt strongly that what he stated was right and would come true. Despite the almost unbearable conditions in the freight car, I had my internal calm. It was the same peace that had come over me earlier in Keszthely when I took my decision not to abandon Father and Mother in order to save myself.

The air was unbearably hot and stifling in the railcar, and the toilet bucket soon ran over. The smell was revolting; all around me people were throwing up. Nonetheless, hunger began to take hold of us. Some spoke ominously of the BBC's inconceivable descriptions of Jewish extermination camps, and fear and despair gripped many. When those voices subsided, someone struck up a song in Yiddish and others joined in within our dark, moving prison with

*Train entrance to Auschwitz-Birkenau, Poland.*

its wretched human cargo. A couple of times chilled water from water hoses at stations rinsed out the railcars and therapeutic water droplets reached our mouths.

Early on the morning of July 8, the train stopped. The sun shone brightly and the air was sparkling when the side door slid open. We had arrived. The place was called Auschwitz. ⇥

# ON THE FRONT LINES, 1944

## Agnes
**July 8, 1944, Auschwitz, Poland**

The morning was bright and sunny when we arrived at Auschwitz. We thought we had come to our POW exchange camp and that the healthy prisoners we saw were those for whom we would be exchanged. I was twenty-five years old, healthy, and vigorous. Positive voices suggested that the war was almost over and that we would probably be exchanged soon. Such were the confusing thoughts that floated among us.

Well-fit prisoners met us and made sure we got off the train. It all happened so quickly. We were pushed down from the boxcars to a platform and placed in lines, different rows for men, women, and women with small children.

*The infamous "Arbeit macht Frei," the gate to Auschwitz-Birkenau.*

In a flash, I saw Father further down in the row beside the one Mother and I were in. I saw him clearly, as he was almost a head taller than the others. He looked over his shoulder, caught my gaze, and shouted out loud to me, "Can you hear me, my girl? Remember what I said, that we will meet there!" pointing at the sky. Mother held my arm tight, saying, "I feel that we must part now, and I don't want to live when we are separated from each other."

The column moved forward, and we held on to each other as tightly as we could. Soon we encountered the doctor, who examined us and motioned for us to join a new column. I realized they had put me in a line with old and weak women. On the other side of the platform were young and healthy girls.

Something seemed to grab hold of me, and I quickly ducked in among the young and healthy girls. Mother remained in the group that was herded away to the gas chambers. Around me one of the girls said, "How did you dare to do that? The girls who tried that earlier were shot at once!" I walked a few steps forward and then stopped in the middle of the crowd. No one around me said a word. A soldier then came, counting us off in tens before he commanded, "Forward, march!"

> In October 1941, the Germans started to build about thirty miles outside the Polish city of Krakow the extermination camp Auschwitz. At the end of the war, the Auschwitz complex contained about three hundred buildings of a planned six hundred, divided into fifty camps and subcamps. The area covered about fifteen square miles. The crematoria for gassing the Jews were found primarily in Auschwitz II-Birkenau, as it came to be known. Many Jews in Birkenau were sent on work gangs to provide slave labor in Germany, and more than 1.1 million Jews were killed in Auschwitz II-Birkenau (Friedländer 2, 539; Bruchefeld and Levine, 53).

*Eight of every ten Hungarian Jews were gassed upon their arrival at Auschwitz.*

We were taken out to a large field where there were already between two hundred and three hundred girls gathered. We were forced to stand until no more women arrived. Then a soldier shouted, "Sit down!" The sun fried us; we were tired, confused, and thirsty.

There was nothing around the field but barracks. We were guarded by twenty soldiers with rifles and fixed bayonets as well as by German Shepherd dogs. They circled around us and appeared very threatening. I lost track of time, but then I finally noticed that it was starting to get dark late in the afternoon or early night. We must have been sitting in that field for six to eight hours. I was in shock. Inside, I sensed the fate that had ended the lives of my mother and father, but I dared not say a word about my thoughts. Later I would find out that Father and Mother were among the

394,000 Hungarian Jews who were sent directly to the gas chambers upon arriving in Auschwitz.

Lost in my thoughts, I was immune to normal pangs of hunger. Then a truck came and dropped off a few large food barrels, and we were each handed a cup and a spoon. The food consisted of a green, cold, vegetable soup. Some never touched it, and some who did threw up. I hesitated but then tasted it. It was like eating hay, but, I thought, hay and vegetables at least had vitamins and the water had been boiled.

Then I heard my father's voice and words inside me. I remembered his blessing. Strengthened by that memory, I decided to fight to stay alive. So, I took a deep breath and forced myself to eat all the food. If I remember right, a surprised soldier came over, looked into my empty cup, and gave me a refill. I ate and drank that, too, and then sat down on the ground again. I now felt a bit strengthened both physically and spiritually. I became determined to do whatever I could to survive and make Father's blessing come true.

No one cared where we sat. The guards said that too many had arrived that day and that they couldn't fit us all into the barracks. Most of the girls stayed put and just lay down on the ground where they were. Some of us sneaked away in the dark. I walked the farthest away and came to some overfilled barracks. Everyone there slept almost on top of each other in the crowded room. In the middle of one of the rooms, I saw an empty spot. Just there, the light came in through the roof. Outside was a full moon and also the spotlights that lit up the area all around the barracks.

> *German concentration camps used trustee inmates who supervised the prisoners. Known as Kapos, these trustees carried out the will of the Nazi camp commandants and guards and were often as brutal as their SS counterparts (Friedländer 2, 546).*

I crawled over about twenty sleeping bodies and lay down flat on my back in the empty spot. The roof above me was open where a few of the roof tiles had fallen off. I looked up at the sky and saw the most beautiful starry night. Nobody had occupied the spot, probably because they didn't want to get wet if it started to rain. But this night was cool, clear, and lovely. I felt gratitude to God that I was able to lie down and stretch out. I knew that both Father and Mother were already dead. Again, I felt a protective power and fell into a deep sleep. ⇒⇐

## Agnes
**July 9, 1944, Auschwitz, Poland**

I woke up to find myself in a cacophony of sound, as the words spoken all around me were foreign. I understood enough to figure out that the girls in the barracks with me were Polish. I understood one of them somewhat, as she spoke to me in Yiddish—a combination of Hebrew and German. She told me that she had been there for two months and had been brought there from a ghetto in Warsaw. She also said that the water truck would come later in the afternoon and that we'd get some food later in the day sometime. All the girls were dirty and very thin, and I thought to myself that I couldn't stay there if I wanted to live. So, I left the barracks and wandered back in the direction of the field.

Soon I stumbled upon a small creek. The water was filthy and muddy, but I drank it anyway. Too late, I saw that the sewer from the barracks emptied into the creek, and a quick thought went through my mind: Now I'll get typhus from the water! But I couldn't even finish that thought before I noticed a barbed wire electric fence, three to four yards high, in front of me. On the other side of the fence stood an old crucifix, the kind used then along roads in the countryside throughout Europe. A few feet from the

*A guard tower and barbed wire fence at Auschwitz.*

crucifix was a tall guard tower, manned by a solitary soldier carrying a rifle and binoculars. He spotted me and shouted, "Achtung, zurück!"

But I acted as if I didn't hear him and knelt next to the fence, facing the crucifix. Then I prayed to Christ. I prayed in a way that felt more like a regular conversation, as if He were actually standing on the other side of the fence, just a few yards away from me. His body was cut out from some kind of metal and was painted as a thin, naked man, wearing only a scant piece of cloth around his waist. The figure was attached to a cross of iron or perhaps cement. When I had completed my prayer, I stood up and looked at the guard above me in the guard tower. He was staring right at me, speechless. He then waved his hand and shouted at me again, and I walked along the fence toward another group of barracks.

As I got closer, I heard Hungarian being spoken. The people shouted and waved at me to hurry. I had wandered into a no-man's land that was guarded by the high-voltage electric fence and armed guards who had shot many people who had previously wandered there or attempted to escape.

The Hungarian barracks were in better condition than the previous one I had been in and occupied by far fewer people. The next morning, the girls there told me that they were going to Birkenau, another barracks city in the large camp, to bathe, get haircuts, and new clothes. They said they were then to be transported in groups of five hundred to different factories in the Third Reich.

Everyone was happy for this chance to survive another few months, and by then, they thought, the war would probably be over. They were all in good physical condition and, until the time of our departure, were given water and a rather good soup, which was served twice a day—half a liter at a time per person, along with a small piece of bread, some margarine, and sausage. Luckily, I was allowed to stay with them, even though I wasn't officially one of the five hundred selected.

The Jewish camp manager was a woman my mother's age who was baffled that I had ended up there "loose," as it was supposed to have been absolutely impossible. I told her about the previous night and about my walk into no-man's land, and she thought that I was insane. I also told her that my mother was from Sopron and that we came from Keszthely. She was from Sopron as well and knew my aunt. Maybe it was for that reason that she hid me among the others in the barracks.

There was no departure the next day, at least not for a change of clothes, haircuts, or bathing. Too many new trains laden with Jews were arriving. It took us two weeks to depart. In the meantime, we heard rumors of more trains arriving by the day, and we began to notice the sickening odor from the large gas chamber ovens and saw the smoke from the great chimneys day and night. Tens of thousands were being cremated, producing a stench that was indescribable. We all understood finally and for sure that our missing kin, old and young, were dead. If someone we knew had somehow managed to get away, we hoped we might find him or her after the war, but now we knew that was unlikely. Strange enough, no one was bitter. Quite the contrary, we were hopeful because we were still alive and not on our way to the gas chambers.

In the barracks, I discovered that I was the only one without a number tattooed on my arm. I asked the girls what the tattoo and its number meant. In wonder, they stared at me. They asked, "How can it be that you don't have a tattoo? They told me that everyone selected for work gangs had received a tattoo immediately after arriving in Auschwitz. Then I realized that the place where I had slept the first night in camp was full of people without tattoos. That meant they were just waiting to be taken to the gas chambers. There were not enough ovens to have immediate room for them, and so they slept a couple of nights in the barracks. Then I knew that when I wandered into no-man's land and prayed in front of the crucifix and walked along the high-voltage fence, it was actually my exodus from Egypt into Israel. The difference was that unfortunately my exodus only dealt with one soul, but Israel's God had heard my father's blessing thus far, and there it was fulfilled.

Once again, I was comforted. Had I remained where I slept the first night, I would have ended up in the gas chambers. I was overcome with a peaceful feeling that I also felt many times during the remaining period of my captivity. ⇒⇐

## Agnes
### July 1944, Birkenau, Poland

After two weeks, it was finally our turn to be bathed and have our heads shaved. We formed up into marching order and began the three-hour trek to the newly built barracks city. When we finally reached the barracks, we were ordered to stop in front of a large building in a meadow. The air was filled with the odor of a disinfected hospital.

We were ordered to remove our clothes and line up in long

rows, naked. The guards went around us and laughed and mocked us. A few guards remained silent and radiated shame and uncertainty. When all of us had removed our clothes, we were led into a large shower with several rows of showerheads, which had both cold and hot water. We were given soap, and it was wonderful to wash myself for the first time in weeks. Then in another room, our heads were shaved again and we received new underwear that smelled like chlorine, as well as some new clothes. I received some striped flannel linen, a pair of wool socks, a burgundy dress, and a pair of cloth boots with wooden soles. I didn't care much for these shoes, and I missed my old ones, which I had been allowed to keep until now. These clothes were, of course, clothes that other prisoners had brought with them in their bundles, the same as we had.

I felt clean and renewed, even if it was a little drafty on my head. Our "new" clothes had a yellow Star of David on their backs.

We were shown to our new barracks at Birkenau, which seemed the lap of luxury compared to the earlier barracks I'd been in. We stayed there four days, waiting to be transported to Bremerhaven, the seaport city of Bremen, where we were supposed to work. In the new barracks, the interior consisted of cubicles on top of one another. Four girls were assigned to each cubicle; it was rather comfortable, even if there were no mattresses. It was like sleeping in a giant wooden box. We were given plenty of food— mostly a vegetable and

*Inside a barracks where the prisoners slept packed together in three levels.*

oatmeal mixture that was like a casserole. In the mornings we got ersatz coffee, bread, and margarine as well as cheese or sausage to put on top. We had free access to cold-water showers. ⋈

## Agnes
**July 1944, Bremen, Germany**

Each of us was given a whole loaf of bread, a half inch of sausage, and nearly a pound of margarine as traveling food when we commenced our journey to our destination at Bremen. There were around five hundred girls. We were counted and told to walk along the railroad siding, where a few boxcars waited for us. I think that we were about fifty in the car. Once again, it was a long way up from the ground to the wooden floor of the freight car. The doors were shut, and we lay down in the dark close to each other on the floor, which was covered with straw. There was just enough room for me to stretch my legs.

We were all excited and in relatively good physical condition. In the beginning, I didn't know anyone in the railroad car. None were from Keszthely or Zalaegerszeg. I had hoped that among the group of fifty at least one person would be from the same area as I was. But that wasn't the case, and in the grand scale of things, I guess it didn't really matter, as we had each lost our family and friends and didn't know what our fate would be.

The train rumbled along for two days and two nights with many stops. Staring out through small peepholes in the side, we took turns describing the landscape to each other. The Orthodox girls sometimes sang Hebrew psalms. Those who were not religious, and even a few Christian girls like me, listened. They have something I don't have, I thought. I understood their faith and hope in the forthcoming Messiah was certain and even fanatical. But in such circumstances, I admired them for it and maybe even envied them.

One night the train stopped at a spooky, quiet city that we discovered was the city of Dresden, Germany, famous for its culture, art, university, zoological garden, and fine porcelain. The rail line was ruined, and we had to march the rest of the way through the city, where the facades of ruined buildings remained somehow majestic and almost whole in the moonlight. Nonetheless, we could see that inside the buildings everything had been destroyed.

We marched until dawn, when we finally reached a train station where the rails had been repaired. There a new train was waiting for us. We were packed in the boxcars in a similar manner as on the previous train and rattled on toward Bremen, where we arrived the following night. Guards were standing on the platform with rifles and the always present German Shepherd dogs. The soldiers yelled at us to do everything faster, which was not easy with so many people pushing and shoving. A few military trucks waited for us, and we were stacked in them, packed like canned sardines. We drove off with such speed that any of us could have fallen over the side at any time. It was a horrific ride, but eventually we arrived without incident at two large barns located next to a giant, modern barracks in a large military base in the port city of Bremen.

We were herded into an old barn that had been fitted with fifty beds, occupying three floors. Everything was fresh and clean. On each bed was a mattress newly stuffed with straw and a neatly folded army blanket. Again, pure luxury compared to Birkenau and Auschwitz. We really were spoiled. I had not had a mattress since the time in the ghetto district of Keszthely. Dead tired, we all fell down on our beds, and I was asleep immediately.

In the morning we were awakened by whistles and ordered to form up in the yard to undergo routine counting and inspection.

Because during the inspection I reported that I could speak and write German, I and four other women were selected to be secretaries. We remained in the meadow all day while the others were out working. Our job was to go through the rooms every morning and write down the names of the women who were sick. In addition, we acted as interpreters between guards and prisoners and collected food for the sick that remained in their beds.

One of the first evenings, several of the girls returned from work with their dresses laden with fresh carrots. I was expected to report this crime, as it was absolutely forbidden to take anything back into the barracks. The carrots had been stolen from allotment gardens outside the wire fence.

It was not long before the garden's shareholder representative arrived and asked to see the camp commandant. I was then called to his office and rudely asked why I had not reported nor confiscated the girls' carrots. I boldly replied that if they had enough food, they would not have stolen. Why, I asked, did we not get the fixed daily diet the documents said that the hard-working women were eligible for? We knew that the guards stole a part of our food.

The camp commandant was angry and upset. He swore at me and told me to leave. A few hours later, he came to me when I was cleaning up. He said that because I was so intelligent and fearless, I would be promoted and become his writing assistant. I replied that I did not want any special status, whether to be his clerk or his mistress.

Then he swore again and said angrily, "Tomorrow you will march out with the others."

"That will be nice," I replied.

The next morning I followed the others out to work. As we passed the gate, soldiers were waiting to accompany us on the way to the day's work assignment. The camp commandant was also there. "Well, are you really going?"

"Yes!" I replied. He kicked the gravel with his boot, turned, and walked away. After that, I followed the others out of camp every day to the work detail.

We worked in a large, half bombed-out factory, producing war matériel. Some stood by the machines, others installed electrical wires in military radios, and still others cleaned and tidied up the drafty, badly damaged industrial building. My job was to clean the toilets and the sinks with soap and water. ⇒·⇐

## *Gustav*

### August 4, 1944, Hallein, Austria

After my furlough and visit home, I returned to Hallein and was sent directly to the eastern front without any proper training. After a failed assassination attack on Hitler in June, orders had been given that all soldiers in reasonable condition should be sent to the front as soon as possible. During my illness and furlough, all Norwegian soldiers had been sent out to the front: the ski battalion to northern Finland and the rest of the soldiers to Estonia. I and one other Norwegian soldier were ordered to take the train and report to Regiment Norway on the Baltic front.

The train arrived at the station in Hallein with a lot of wheezing and hissing from the steam engine. To get on board and secure a seat, passengers on the platform pushed and shoved as the train decelerated. We were naïve enough to believe that we would get comfortable seats and be able to sleep. On the train all the lights were dimmed and the dark aisles were quickly filled with people who did not have seats.

My fellow soldier had saved a half-finished bottle of wine that smelled bad and tasted worse. But the wine was good enough to celebrate our last day in a non-war-torn country and to make us therapeutically drunk. Lacking any glasses, he distributed the wine among people on the train, pouring it into their cooking utensils.

In the darkness and congestion, we stumbled across a man who was sleeping on the floor. Next to him we found a reasonably free floor space where we could throw down a small rug. We sipped on the remaining drops of wine, but our celebration never really got started.

On the railway platform in Munich, we met a Norwegian soldier whose leg had been amputated; he was on his way home. He had spent nineteen months in a hospital in Vienna where he was treated for a gunshot wound in his leg. We sent letters home to our families with him. We figured that the letters would arrive home uncensored and faster that way.

In the afternoon of the same day, we were fortunate enough to get seats on the train from Leipzig that would take us to Berlin. The train screeched on at a high speed, but I felt that time passed slowly. The sky was clear, and the moon rose high, round, and yellow. I fell asleep to the monotonous thump of the train and sank into a deep sleep.

In my dream I heard thunder and was awakened by the noise. Around me soldiers were crawling on the floor. Everyone tried to protect himself as best he could. A sharp, acrid smell filled the air. Through the window I could see small flashes of light that regularly came at us at very high speed from a hill about a hundred yards from the embankment. The train cars were hit with one explosion after another. The explosions got weaker and weaker the farther away from the hill the train moved. It was a large-caliber machine gun that fired at us. As it was, losses were confined to four wounded soldiers and numerous bullet holes in the railcars.

For us it was incomprehensible that such an assault could take place so far inside Germany. It did not match the military bulletins with which we were constantly inundated in Hallein.

The train had not slowed its speed during the shooting but continued onward. None of those responsible for rail traffic came into the train to see what had happened. The four wounded soldiers received first aid from other soldiers and stayed with us all the way to Leipzig. The shooting was but an unnoticed little scene in a vast and seemingly endless tragedy. It was the first time—but far from the last—that I experienced someone shooting at me. The rest of the train travel was without enemy shooting, and finally we reached our destination near the Baltic front in the eastern part of Estonia, close to Narva. I was to become a soldier in 11th SS Division Nordland, Regiment Norway, 2nd battalion, 5th company. ❧❧

## Gustav

### August 31, 1944, the Baltic front, east of Narva, Estonia

On August 31, 1944, we were ordered to pack our gear and with our weapons in hand prepare to march off to the front. We each had about sixty pounds, maybe more, to carry. The whole company, 140 men, lined up in platoons. We were trained and ready. The company commander, a lieutenant, spoke to us and explained that the longer movements would normally use trucks to transport troops and their equipment. Unfortunately, however, no trucks were available. We had a fifteen-mile march in front of us. Those forced to carry ammunition protested but to no avail.

A soldier to my right dropped his pack from pure fear when he heard the lieutenant's message. That soldier had just been released from the hospital a few days earlier and had not had time to recover his strength. He collapsed on the ground and cried. By this time, though, we each had enough problems caring for ourselves and were indifferent to his burdens.

The marching order consisted of two columns, one on each side of the road. Between each man in a column was to be a distance of seven to eight feet. We had to carry all our equipment with us. At 3:00 in the afternoon an NCO took command, and the march began.

During the first few miles, one could hear a lot of complaints and cursing in different languages. Gradually, the complaints diminished. We soldiers had enough to contend with—our heavy packs, the pace we had to keep, sore shoulders, and increasingly tired legs. After seven and a half miles, we received orders to take a break and lie down. The order to lie down was unnecessary; everyone threw himself quickly to the ground with legs raised to avoid cramps.

The march continued as darkness fell. The August darkness thickened, and the terrain became more rugged. Every now and then we would hear an angry outburst as someone tripped over a rock or a tall tuft of grass and then fell with his pack. It was only with some difficulty that anyone was able to get up carrying his heavy pack. Our proximity to the front lines meant danger if anyone wandered off and lost his bearings. In front of us, up over the forest, we saw flares and light signals, which rose and fell. And we listened to the crackle of rifle and machine-gun fire ahead of us. Looking skyward in the darkness, we could see the tops of shattered trees that had been blasted by artillery fire. Our path wound its way between the puddles that often ran into each other, and we had to detour around them to avoid getting wet. To make matters worse, it began to rain.

Finally, we received orders to halt. All of us soldiers dropped to the ground. We lay like bundles here and there among the roots and clumps of small bushes. For the final few miles, our march discipline had completely failed. Our NCO passed word from man to man that there should be dugouts for us to shelter in. Some of us searched for openings to the dugouts. One of us crawled into a dark hole but soon came flying out again. There were already soldiers in there who were not pleased to be awakened by an intruder.

Those inside might have thought my colleague was a Russian who sneaked in, and they beat him up before throwing him out of their hole. The soldier who was thrown out was just grateful he had not been shot. We continued to search, and one by one we found a bunker or the opening to a protected pit that was deep enough to provide a false sense of security. Seven soldiers managed to squeeze into a cramped bunker.

I was tormented by a terrible thirst and could not resist the temptation to drink the water I found in a black puddle, though I knew I should not do it. The water tasted awful, and the taste, more than the water itself, drove away the urge to drink. I did not manage to force my way into a bunker for protection but instead crawled into a thicket and made of twigs a primitive shield against the rain. I fell asleep from exhaustion amidst the foliage.

The sun was high in the sky when I was awakened by the cold. Half asleep and still thirsty, I went to the pool of water from which I had tried to drink the previous night, thinking perhaps it would taste better now. It was a puddle formed in a shell hole. On its edge lay a dead Russian soldier. It appeared that the corpse had lain there for several days. All desire to drink from that pool of water disappeared immediately.

I sat on a rock and surveyed the surrounding, war-torn landscape, and I thought morosely, "It is here I shall either live or die." It seemed that only a few months ago there had been a dense, deciduous forest, which now was reduced to stumps, broken treetops, and blackened, burned tree trunks. All the trees were shattered, some at the ground. Other trees were split open all the way down to the roots. Scores of trees were ripped out with their roots pointing skyward. The ground was pocked with shell holes, which ran into each other. And everywhere were dead Russian soldiers. Here and there a Russian rifle pointed into the air. A few abandoned, burnt-up Russian tanks riddled with bullet holes completed the

*The Soviet Union deployed Katyusha rocket launchers, which delivered a large quantity of explosives at once.*

image of total chaos. The view from my rock on the hill was, at the very least, a melancholy scene. I had arrived at the Baltic front. ⇒⇐

## Gustav

September 1944, the Baltic front, east of Narva, Estonia

Our trenches began in a narrow belt of forest and eventually followed a path out of a bog. Our group's assignment appeared to be to defend the position farthest from the company bunker. The trench was in many places narrow and difficult to move in. In addition, rain and artillery shells had nearly destroyed its walls. In front of our trenches was the bog, which drifted toward a hill. Our foxhole had been strengthened and excavated to a depth of three yards and nearly three yards wide. The walls were reinforced with timber and mud. In one place the wooden walls had been destroyed by a direct hit by enemy artillery.

The first casualty came one night when three men were sent out on a reconnaissance mission. They were to sneak over to the Russian front lines and attempt to learn what they could. It was a dangerous assignment, but any facts might come in handy when we launched an attack. As the soldiers climbed over the edge of their foxhole, a random shot hit one of them in the head, and he died at the first-aid station.

After a week, things got livelier as the Russians increased their mortar fire. All our time was with filled with work as we repaired the damage being done to our defensive structure. Officers supervised and inspected our work. One of them was heard to say that he thought the Russian thrust would be aimed at our position. True or not, we were motivated to shore up our defenses.

As we worked, we weren't allowed to assemble in groups when we spoke together. The few times we did, an officer was immediately there, shouting at us. Our artillery also increased its activity hour by hour. During the night, we often heard "the bellowing cow," a heavy German multiple-rocket launcher named Wurfrahmen 40, which had gotten its name from the terribly loud sound it produced

*The German Wurfrahmen 40, introduced in 1940, launched 300mm high-explosive rockets but was less accurate than conventional artillery.*

when its rockets were fired. The sound might better be described as the sound of a rusty door hinge but a hundred times worse. The first sign these rockets gave was a flash across the sky; then came the terrible sound. After it was fired, all became quiet along the front line, as the Russians took cover and the Germans waited to see the results of the impact. Then our side would fire off more rockets, which climbed over the treetops in a burning, climbing, circular arch. As they climbed, the rocket produced a bright red trail, which was extinguished as it began its downward trip to the calculated target.

It was important for our soldiers to quickly seek protection from incoming rockets. Ideally, one would crawl like a weasel into a hole or along the bottoms of trenches to avoid shrapnel and dramatic changes in air pressure. If a rocket landed in soft ground, a pillar of dirt and smoke would climb straight up into the air, and everything near the impact site would be destroyed. After the explosions, the ground would shake and then a tremor would run through the ground.

A few minutes after the bellowing cow had done its work, soldiers returned to their normal activity at the front. Initially, random shots would be fired here and there. They were then followed by regular, rattling, machine-gun rounds. Then calm would again descend in our front lines. As long as the activity was at a normal level, we could feel fairly at ease. Then we knew that the enemy was not out and moving toward our trenches. If there was total silence for a few long minutes, we could expect anything. Each of us would be on tenterhooks, analyzing any suspicious sounds and trying to see through the darkness. ⇒⋅⋲

## Gustav

**September 23, 1944, the Baltic front, Dobele, south of Riga, Latvia**

We six new arrivals were ordered to be the first to attack the Russian front. We would have enemy artillery and machine guns firing at us from the front and, at the same time, tanks firing from behind us. We were to break through the Russian line and defeat them.

> *The Russians attempted to split the German Army Group North close to Dobele, south of Rīga, Latvia. The Nordland Division was moved from Estonia and ordered to stop the Russians. Both Nordland Division Regiment Norway and Nordland Division Regiment Denmark attacked the Russians near Dobele September 22–25, 1944 (Tieke, 121).*

But our task was suicide, plain and simple, and we new arrivals had been cynically chosen. Our thankless task was to entice the Russians to shoot at us. Our tanks would then see where the Russians were positioned and open fire on them.

To fortify our nerves, our NCO offered us a special drink before the attack and saw to it that we drank it all. The narcotic drink was supposed to lower our anxiety, but it also made me fuzzy-headed and gave me tunnel vision.

With our weapons off safety, our little drugged group was ready to go. A flare signaling the attack sizzled up into the sky and exploded in dazzling white fireworks. Our tanks drove into the small valley up the hill and toward where the Russians were. My comrades and I ran out into no-man's land in front of and around the tank. In the frontline battle, we did not strap our steel helmets under the chin. Air pressure from an exploding shell could rip our heads off.

When we stormed down the hill, my steel helmet flew off. Gunshots. Alarm. Tank noise. Heartbeats. Running toward death. I was almost down in the valley when a flash thought ordered me to move one step to the right. I did that and immediately felt a sharp slap on my cheek. Blood ran down onto my machine gun, which soon became completely red colored. I was running in front of the tank, however, and the wound in my face did not cause me to stop. Then bang! I felt it in my left thigh. The bang sounded like an inflated balloon being pricked, but I ran still farther. From the front the enemy machine guns shot constantly at us, and from the back our tank fired its deadly guns toward the Russian positions.

*Forest and tanks at the Baltic front.*

From hip position I constantly shot my machine gun, kept running in front of the tank, and climbed a knoll. Hardly a minute later, suddenly the tank and I were inside the Russian front line. The tanks had done their job: the noise of the tank engines had frightened the Russians, and when they tried to run, the tank's guns shot them over our heads. Slain Russian soldiers, still clinging to their weapons, lay sprawled in their foxholes. I saw a Russian who was trying to escape into the woods. He was shot by an unknown soldier and fell forward headlong. As though in a fog, I saw one last Russian sitting among the trees.

After the breakthrough, my left leg suddenly became stiff, and I looked for the other machine gunner. He had sought refuge behind a large tree. Despite his protests, I forced him to take my machine gun.

The attack had been successful. Many of our soldiers came in through the gap that we and the tank had created in the Russian defensive line. Company soldiers streamed through the gap to "roll up" the front. Among them were the German soldiers who had been at the front before we arrived.

I don't know what happened to all of my five comrades. I later learned that one other had also survived. I know nothing about the fate of the others, but I had survived my baptism of fire at the front.

After the breakthrough, the artillery took up their positions. Everyone knew his duty and did it perfectly in the spirit of German order. Everyone worked quickly and quietly. Several soldiers helped apply first-aid bandages to my face and left thigh.

I think the more seasoned soldiers looked at us newcomers with two different attitudes. First, they probably saw us as novices who did not understand what to expect. Second, they looked at us with gratitude that we would carry out such a deadly mission, which they had avoided. Being behind the front lines and behind a tank were, after all, easier than storming into enemy fire with a tank behind you firing directly over your head.

I pulled myself to my feet. I needed to get to the company's medical station as quickly as possible. After the medics had categorized me and then attended to me, I received shots against cramps and fever from my wounds. The medics cleaned my wounds and dressed them with white bandages on my thigh and over my cheek. One bullet had ripped open a long flesh wound on my face.

---

*During peace negotiations in the spring of 1944, the Soviets demanded that Finland surrender unconditionally and allow Soviet troops to occupy Finland. Had that happened, Finland would have become part of the Soviet Union, with the Iron Curtain brought westward to the boundary between Sweden and Finland. In the event, however, German troops held firm in the Narva region of Estonia from June to August 1944 and inflicted heavy losses on the Russians. In response, the Soviet Union changed their terms. Finland signed the peace treaty on September 4, 1944, thereby avoiding becoming part of the Soviet-controlled Eastern Bloc ("Andra Världskriget," 203; Tieke, 81).*

Another had gone almost straight through my left leg. An army ambulance was quickly loaded, and we drove wobbling away.

Lying in a hospital bed, I again mentally recounted my first direct encounter with the enemy. My vision was limited and certainly influenced by the concoction I had been ordered to drink. As best I could from hip position, I had fired my machine gun all the way. Around me and in the air: bang swisch-wiiiiii tat tat tat—bang wiiiiii.

Noise, bangs, and explosions had been unspeakably violent. As sure as I lived, I could have been dead. I also clearly remembered feeling ordered by someone during my attack to take a step to the right. Which I did. That probably saved the bullet from hitting me directly in the face. Instead it just nicked my left cheek.

A few days later I was awarded a medal for having been wounded in battle. Then I was ordered to take whatever military equipment I still had and prepare to return to the front. ⇒⇐

*Medal for being wounded in battle.*

## Agnes
**September 1944, Bremen, Germany**

One morning at 8:00 we, as usual, were packed on a flatbed truck and were on our way to the factory when the air raid alarm sounded. Everyone rushed to the large bunker that looked like a concrete skyscraper without windows. Those of us who were Jewish, with a large Star of David on our backs, were not allowed to take shelter in the bunker. Instead, the truck took us to a park. Our guards became completely hysterical because they could not seek shelter in the bunker. Bombs rained down around us, building facades collapsed, fires started, and we felt very vulnerable. One of us found a descending slope in the middle of the park's lawn. Probably there had once been a public toilet below ground level. We rushed down the slope and into some sort of small room, but inside the walls had collapsed and it was impossible to move forward through all the rubble and gravel. We pushed ourselves in as best we could, smelling smoke and listening to the bombers that thundered over us. The guards were deathly pale and shaking with fear.

Some Orthodox believers began to sing in Hebrew Jewish hymns from the Psalms. Those of us who could not sing were completely silent. In spite of the confusion and destruction, with my eyes closed, I felt a reverence as if I were in a large cathedral. After three hours, we ventured out of the abandoned and crumbling public toilet. We saw no sign of life, and everywhere were fires in the bombed-out houses. Smoke billowed out from small openings in the concrete skyscraper. The bunker was completely blackened. We cast our eyes over the lawn in the park and saw some small impact pits and piles of gravel, but that was all. We were all unharmed.

To get through the collapsed and burning buildings took more than five hours. Later, we learned that the blackened concrete skyscraper had been hit by heavy bombs. Several hundred people had suffocated in the bunker where we had been refused entry. When we at last arrived at the factory, we found just smoke and ruins. With the guards looking after us, we took long detours back to the camp where we found our barracks completely intact.

For two days we did not leave the camp. Then we were reorganized into smaller groups of twenty-five. Shovels were distributed, and we had to go out to the streets of Bremen and create a small path through the rubble in the road so traffic could start moving again. It was quite dangerous to work near buildings with unstable, half-collapsed facades. Now and then we heard a strong boom as a facade fell down, creating a huge dust cloud. Eventually we were sent back to the factory again. ⇥⇤

> *The British general Sir Arthur Harris focused on massive bombing on civilian targets to try to break civilian resistance. The American Air Force general Carl Spaatz had another strategy, to focus the bombing not on civilians but on the oil industry, which would affect the ability of the German forces to move. The Bremen area was a center of oil-related industries ("Andra Världskriget," 42).*

## Gustav

September 1944, the Baltic front, Dobele, near Riga, Latvia

I was once again on the front line. How long could I cope with such a life? As before, I was assigned to a machine-gun nest. My machine gun was damaged, however, and would be returned to service the following day. Until then my comrade and I were to manage with only our rifles.

By suppertime, orders came that my group should cross into Russian territory and, if possible, capture an enemy soldier. It fell to my lot to stand guard alone out in no-man's land waiting for the return of my comrades. Usually such an assignment involved two soldiers with machine guns and grenades. Since my machine gun was broken, I had only my rifle and fifteen extra rounds. I went to my post, worrying about my inadequate equipment, but then thought how long the front line was and how small the chance was of the Russians attacking right then and there.

Soon I discovered that my judgment was worthless. My guard post was at a so-called advanced position only some fifty yards from the Russian line.

Alone out there in the darkness, I tried to hear every sound that broke the silence. I was extremely nervous and would surely have heard if only one little twig was broken on the side facing the Russian front. But it was treacherously quiet and peaceful until, suddenly, I heard a few muffled grenade explosions and the clatter of automatic rifle fire and machine guns. Then it became quiet again.

I tried in vain to penetrate the darkness with my eyes. I still feared the darkness of night, and the first rays of morning light always provided me with a sense of relief. Not being able to see if there were hostile Russian soldiers only a few feet away was, to say the least, nerve racking. I did not yet realize that the enemy soldiers had similar feelings. It would take several months before I realized that the perils of the night were small compared with the dangers that lurked in the light of day.

A few minutes later, I heard stealthy steps and saw members of my group coming back across the bog. We managed to identify one another without opening fire by mistake. The group thought they found a Russian position, but when they approached it, they found it empty. Half an hour later, I was relieved and laboriously made my way back to our company. In the pitch-black autumn night, it was not so easy to follow the trails that traversed the woods.

Just when I got back, orders came that we were to move again. Then, for some reason, the movement order was postponed until the next day. We needed no more than ten minutes to pack and make ourselves ready, but now we had to wait twenty-four hours. That meant that I got one more night of guard duty alone outside in the dark forest swamp.

In the darkest part of the night, I heard someone moving close to me. It must be a Russian reconnaissance patrol, I thought. I weighed what I would do in my mind. Then, in the clearing in front of me, I glimpsed one, two, three silhouettes against the sky, moving along the front. It was nonsense for me to fire at them—they certainly had machine guns, and I had only a rifle. Suddenly they turned and came straight towards my position. Now they were not more than fifteen yards away from me.

I forgot all about calling for the password, or maybe I did not dare. I no longer had a choice. I lifted my rifle. A glimmer of light, a crack of my rifle, and a scream. The silence was broken. Above the cries of the wounded soldier, I heard some shouts in German but with a foreign accent. They also shouted out the watchword for that night. Then I understood. In front of me were Latvian soldiers. But what were they doing in the darkness beyond our front line? The wounded man was cursing and screaming, but his comrades assisted him, and all three withdrew. It then became calm at the front again, though I was certainly not so calm.

It was not long until a sergeant came to my post. The incident had been reported, and he wanted to get a detailed report from me. Had I fallen asleep? I explained that I had been awake and on edge throughout my guard duty. He then told me the men I had seen belonged to a Latvian unit that would take over from us the next day. They had been told to familiarize themselves with the front sector in advance of that takeover. There was, however, a bit of luck amidst the misfortune in that my machine gun was broken. Otherwise, the three would not have escaped so lightly. ⇥

## *Gustav*

### October 1944, the Baltic front, Priekule, Latvia

It was expected that the Russians would make a heavy assault on our part of the front. My foxhole was in a lower part of the terrain with slopes on all sides except in the front. We dug in as well as we could. Russian grenades and artillery shells started hitting the whole area. We heard noise from tank engines behind us. We understood that the grenades coming from behind were from Russian tanks. My companion shouted, "Look behind!" About seventy-five yards away were twenty to twenty-five advancing Russians. We sent a machine-gun burst in their direction. There were also Russians to our front, and they were starting to shoot at us. We were trapped and had to regroup.

Carrying the machine gun and the ammunition, we ran back as fast as we could. From a corner of a house, a Russian with a machine gun fired at us. A wounded German soldier behind us shouted for help. We could not stop. Rounds hit the ground all around us. I heard a sound of metal being hit by a bullet. My companion's helmet flew past me, and he fell to the ground. I luckily was able to make it back to the company headquarters. ⇒·⇐

## Gustav

### October 1944, the Baltic front, Priekule, Latvia

There was no longer a front line to speak of. We were ordered to dig foxholes and defend ourselves no matter where we were. I found an old shovel in a farmyard, crawled into a ditch, and dug frantically. The Russians had discovered us and fired constantly at our puny foxholes.

As I dug, the tops of my shoulders and my bowed head were intermittently visible above the edge of the foxhole. Instantly I came under fire. I threw myself down on the ditch bottom and pushed myself flat against the ground. Soon the firing ceased, and I tried to use my shovel to dig deeper into the ditch bottom. This scene was repeated again and again. After several failed attempts to dig deeper, I crawled out of the hole and managed to slip down behind a haystack before the Russians could begin to shoot again.

Getting out of the foxhole turned out to be better than just

*A machine-gunner SS soldier in a foxhole at the Baltic front.*

lying there on its bottom. The Russians had advanced well forward to the corner of the farmer's house. But we could hold them off as long as they only attacked from the front. It was much more difficult when they began to encircle the entire farm. At most, we were ten uninjured defenders. Some Russians had already breached our flank, and an attack from the rear was expected soon. A sergeant asked if anyone wanted to volunteer to follow him and drive the Russians out. Along with five or six others, I volunteered and went with the NCO. No sooner had we left our positions than the supposedly safe farmhouse came under heavy artillery fire. Those who had remained behind were killed.

We hurried along a deep trench. We saw Russian troops running between the neighboring farmhouses. Then we heard the rumble of big engines. Was it the Russian T-34 tanks? As the rumble increased in volume, it became music to our ears: German tanks were on the way forward to our rescue. An officer from a neighboring company had a few men. They and four tanks moved to counterattack and drove the Russians back. We joined them, staying close to the tanks. Together we pushed the enemy back and away from the area around the farms. We had carried out our orders. The Russian thrust was stopped!

German artillery had not fired a single shot all day. Having been on the move, they were unable during the previous night to set up and target the guns before the Russian assault. Therefore, the infantry had had to operate without artillery support throughout the day. We had repelled the enemy attack on our section of the front with nothing but small arms plus the saving support of four tanks that finally arrived.

I later learned that all our company and platoon officers died that day, and the Russians very nearly broke through the line. I later received an Iron Cross second class for my participation in repelling the Russian offensive. ⇒⋲

## Gustav

**October 1944, the Baltic front, Priekule, Latvia**

Our machine gun barely fit in our small dugout. When nothing was happening, I slept curled up at one end of it. Suddenly I was awakened by a series of strange sounds: bang-swish, wham-swish, bang-swish. I could hear them again and again over our dug-in position.

My comrade had stood guard in our dugout and kept an eye on the surrounding area. When the sun rose on the edge of the horizon and daylight broke upon us, it was time for me to take over the watch. The strange sounds continued; they were quite uncommon. Now and then small pine branches fell to the earth when hit by errant projectiles. An explosion slapped the trees above my head, and then came the swishing sound of the shell in the air. My companion, whom I had relieved, was already deeply asleep despite the gunfire.

Shells continued to hit the earth all around us. Some shells hit our position but did little more than cause a fire. I saw smoke rising up from the front of our location, the side that faced the Russians. In my state of heightened tension, I was curi-

*Waiting for the enemy.*

ous what was causing the smoke. Without permission, I left my assigned spot. The frame supporting part of the dugout was covered in flames, and there was nothing to do but put them out. I took a bushy branch, struck the flames with three mighty blows, and put out the fire. For some reason, I was not in any great hurry to leave there, so I waited until I was sure the frame had not caught fire again.

The Russians stopped shooting, and I heard one of them yell in broken German, "Comrade, come over to us. You will be treated well here. This is where you get good food and beds with white sheets to sleep in. Don't worry about your leaders. If they try to stop you, shoot them!" The Russian soldier repeated his offer several times before he withdrew.

I did not think much about it right then, but I soon realized it was strange that I had thoughtlessly left my position to put out a fire and the Russians hadn't shot me.

## *Gustav*

### October 1944, the Baltic front, Priekule, Latvia

For several days we held our position on top of a hill. A brook ran a few feet below the crest and beyond it was a plain. In the other direction, the hill sloped downward to a field with at least half a mile of open ground. Here and there were abandoned farmhouses. We felt undisturbed in our position and even relaxed between guard duty hours. We slept, ate food, rested, and watched.

It was not possible to sleep in tents or under a roof, however. We always slept in the position we occupied. Often it was in a hole that we had dug. If the ground was impossible to dig in, we built up a bulwark of stone and timber or other available materials. We were a replacement group, so usually others had dug in and put up a framework before we arrived. It was different during attack or retreat, though. The work was often performed during the night to provide protection during the stressful day to come.

The continuous stay outdoors had no negative effect on me. Even in the winter, being outdoors did not bother me, neither frost, nor cold, nor precipitation. When it became real winter, we wore padded winter uniforms, which were thicker than summer uniforms, yet equally pliable. And we were equipped with warm blankets and boots as well.

The leaves on the trees turned autumn-colored and began to fall. I slept a great deal. It did not matter whether it was day or night; whenever I didn't have to stand guard, I slept.

One morning in October, I was standing guard in our position on top of the hill when two Russian soldiers in long winter coats and pointy hats came stumbling over another hill dragging a machine gun. They were clearly visible about 350 yards from me. I interpreted the event as their having been given permission to leave their designated position to participate in some shooting practice. They were still a ways from me, and there were probably other German soldiers closer to them than I was. Surely they would open fire if necessary. I let the two continue undisturbed.

Apparently they were totally unaware of where the front line ran between the Russians and the Germans. The Germans did not

know, either. Consequently, the Russians passed our sector unde-
tected and disappeared behind a hill. After a while I heard them
firing their machine gun. The bursts of gunfire created near-panic
in a group of German gunners who were not prepared for battle.
The German artillerymen gathered their horses together in a panic
and retreated at full gallop to a secure place in a nearby forest. ⇒⇐

# BLESSINGS AMIDST SUFFERING, 1944–1945

*Agnes*
**October 1944, Bremen, Germany**

It rained frequently, and the temperature fell. It was cold, and we were freezing. We had no socks, no hair on our heads, and nothing to put on our heads to help protect us from the cold. Many had the flu, and all of us were constantly hungry. The bad camp soup we received in the evenings was not enough to satisfy our hunger.

Among our guards were two Hungarian-speaking soldiers. They belonged to the German minority in Hungary and had been forced to join the SS. One of them was especially nice. He had been assigned to our group, and with his collusion, we were allowed to search through the ruins to find anything that was useful. We soon became experts at finding clothes under the rubble. We climbed the ruined mounds, dug our way down to the cabinets and closets, and salvaged whatever we could find.

Once I found a chest of drawers that contained a lot of socks. I put on four pair, one on top of the other, so that my shoes fit better and my legs were no longer blue from the cold. A piece of cloth I found in a closet became a scarf for my shaved head. One Sunday I sewed a jacket from a quilt I found. I wore it under my thin summer coat, and in that way I was better dressed for winter. We learned that many houses had a solid concrete basement room that resisted bombing attacks. We were able to dig down through basement windows to these rooms that were hidden under the rubble. Of course, it was strictly forbidden to steal from the food supplies we found, but our Hungarian guards looked the other way, and we were able to scrounge for ourselves.

We ate jams, pickles, and even barrels of herring. The guard allowed himself to be bought off—these were delicacies, even for him. One day we came to a big dairy that had been destroyed by bombs. The milk we found in some bottles had gone sour, but the fire that followed the bombing had caused the milk in other bottles to boil and become cheese. It was nutritious and tasted really good. In the egg store next door, we found a variety of hard-boiled eggs that had been cooked by the fire's heat. We needed only to take all this bounty. It was not manna from heaven, but it was given to us almost like the Israelites had received their manna. In this way we were saved from starving to death. ⇒⇐

## Agnes
### November 1944, Bremen, Germany

As part of our cleanup duties and to reduce the risk of being harmed by buildings suddenly collapsing on us, we had to pull down bombed-out facades before we could clean up the streets. We would hook a rope into the empty windows by one of us climbing up the fallen bricks or debris that reached up to the first window. By having all twenty-five of us in our group simultaneously pull on the heavy rope, it was relatively easy to pull down an empty facade. When the facades were pulled down, they spread their brick dust and cement over the streets, and we could clear narrow

*A heavily bombed area in Bremen, Germany, 1945.*

streets without fear. For three weeks reaching into the first part of
November we worked clearing streets.

Then came the night when the bombs rained down all over
Bremen. From our barracks we looked out and could see fire
everywhere. Our barracks were hit, and I heard someone yelling
that one end was burning. In our room the women ran around in
complete panic and hysteria and pushed against the locked door.
It gave way, and they exited into a dark corridor. There the screams
continued. I lay quietly in my bed and prayed fervently to God for
help. To the girl in the bed under me, I said, "Lie still! We don't
want to be trampled to death by our own in the corridor." Then we
two walked to the window overlooking the backyard and opened it.

"If a fire starts in the hallway or if there is heavy smoke," I said to the girl, "then we will just climb out and wait in the back."

Small bombs rained down in front of us in the backyard and set the grass on fire. We waited. The screams in the corridor grew in intensity, but after about ten minutes the guards shoved everyone back into their rooms. Then came the signal for all clear.

The next morning we learned that two young Polish women had been trampled to death in the panic, and many were injured, some with life-threatening injuries. We also saw that the American and British bomber formations had performed their tasks with great precision. All around us were burnt-out neighborhoods, but our barracks with the Red Cross insignia painted on it was unharmed, except for where the gables had caught fire. The fire wardens had managed to quickly extinguish it. Close to our barracks, more than thirty thousand people were killed in a previously undamaged neighborhood.

That day we were ordered to a different street from "our street" and "our shop" where we had been able to acquire cheese and eggs. We were taken to the clearing in front of a huge bunker that contained a hospital. The bunker was unharmed, but the sick were nonetheless evacuated. They were on stretchers and had caretakers with them as they were carried out of the bunker. We shoveled on as best we could in order to help the stretcher bearers come out. I don't know if the sick and wounded were civilians or soldiers.

We were also shocked to see confused and panic-stricken people running around and writing messages on the remains of their houses. They would write who they were and where they intended to go. Anguished faces testified that they feared that relatives had been caught under the rubble and were not yet out of danger. Soldiers pushed or carried away screaming people who were in shock.

Later, we were moved to a nearby neighborhood where we knocked gravel and cement from bricks. We stacked them in nice and straight lines to be used in reconstruction, though with the war continuing, any hope of rebuilding was just an absurd parody.

One morning a nice little boy about three years old came carrying a toy shovel in his hand. He was completely uninjured. He started digging in the cold pile of ruins.

"What are you doing?" I asked.

"I have to dig up my mother."

It had been four days since the bombing attack. No one knew where he came from or how it was that he was completely unharmed. Had he wandered around alone since then? How could he be in such good condition? We wanted to embrace and comfort the boy. But before we were able to, the soldiers came. The boy disappeared from our sight, bundled in the arms of a large soldier. I really hope that he survived. Oh, this terrible war! What traumatic events and days for that boy and so many others. ⇒⋅⇐

## Gustav
### October 1944, the Baltic front, Priekule, Latvia

We came from different countries—Norway, Sweden, Denmark, Finland, Germany, Bulgaria, Hungary, Czechoslovakia, Holland, Belgium, and Italy. We were young men and volunteer soldiers of the Waffen-SS. What had brought us together? If someone had asked us, I think the answers would have included idealism, perhaps the communist threat, or perhaps simply seeking adventure. We should have discussed these issues among ourselves, but the subject very rarely surfaced. We were too involved in the battle at hand or in the struggle to survive, or we were so tired that we could not be bothered to talk to each other.

> *When the Soviet army failed to break through the German lines at Dobele, south of Rīga, in Latvia, they focused their forces on the southern part of the front, close to Priekule. The Soviets intended to take the harbor of Liepāja to cut off supplies to the whole German Army Group North. Because Nordland was seen as a strong unit, they were moved to that area to stop the advancing Soviets (Tieke, 122–24).*

During one retreat we were forced to travel in an overcrowded and uncomfortable truck bed, and we ended up sleeping in the most amazing positions. One soldier was lying with his head dangling off the side of the truck, but we paid him no attention since we didn't meet any vehicles going in the opposite direction. I found a place on the roof of the truck's cab, my legs hanging over the side of the truck and my hands clinging to the iron bar that attached the tarp to the bed when the bed was covered. There I sat and thought of how tired I was and repeatedly wondered if it was dangerous to sit as I did. But I eventually gave in to my fatigue and fell asleep.

I awoke to the sound of men yelling but was not immediately aware of what was happening. By now the night was pitch black. I stretched my arm out and felt the ground. Something was pushing against my legs, and the pressure increased. Now I was wide awake. My legs were pinned under the cab, and the truck was balanced in such a way that it could at any moment fall on its side and crush me.

The pain, coupled with my intense desire to get out of there, made me cry out so the others who had fallen off the bed of the truck spotted me and my predicament. In the darkness, they gathered around the vehicle and tried to lift the cab to free my legs. The first attempt failed. They released the cab, and in their so doing, the weight of the cab's frame pressed even harder against my legs. I gave a loud shriek that encouraged my colleagues to try again.

This time the cab was lifted sufficiently that two soldiers managed to pull me out from under it. They stood me up, and the NCO in charge wanted to see if I could stand on my own. Stumbling like a newborn calf, I took a few steps. When my legs held me upright, I was quite relieved, even though the pain was very severe. The incident left a mark across one shin for several years. ❧

## Agnes
### November 1944, Bremen, Germany

We were so undernourished that most of the time we only pretended to work. We did not have the strength to do a full day's work, and we were constantly tired. After the work day was over, we returned to camp in the dark, traveling by train and then by truck; then we marched the final stretch to a puny meal and instantly fell asleep. At 9:00, we had to be silent.

The rooms were small, and eight girls shared each room, stacked into bunk beds. By the foot of each bed was a small stool, and in the middle of the floor stood a military iron stove with a washbasin attached to it. Each girl had a deep metal dish, a steel bucket, a cup, and a spoon. Other than our clothing, that was all our furnishings and personal equipment.

One day, we came to a street that was completely destroyed on one side, but the other was untouched and still populated. The untouched side even had a bread store, which was open for business. Once an old man walked by and threw something on the ground in front of me. Then he hurried into the store, which was forbidden territory for us.

I looked down and saw a piece of paper. I picked it up. Wrapped inside were some bread coupons and a few coins. I thanked God and thought that this was more manna from heaven. When the guards and the rest of the girls were busy working on the other side of the street and they could not see me, I ran as fast as I could into the bread shop. Inside, I saw a terrified old woman standing behind the counter. We were all alone. I handed her the coupons and the money and received a whole loaf of bread in return.

I then took courage and started to talk to her, explaining who we were and where we came from. All of a sudden, she began to cry and said that she and her friends would do everything in their power to help us while we were there. She said she had heard of work camps and prisoners nearby but was shocked to hear about Auschwitz and that her country treated people in such a shameful way in the camps.

As I told her more about the concentration camps, she continued to cry and asked for my forgiveness; she wanted me to know that all Germans were not the same. I felt she wanted to help us but knew that if she did so, the guard would take her and maybe put her with us. So I told her not to do anything. I ate a part of the bread, hid what was left under my jacket, and then sneaked back onto the street. Just as I left, two people approached the store, but I managed to get out before they saw my face. Well outside, I ran as fast as I could back to the spot where my group was working. When I returned, a guard asked me where I had been, and I told him I had been looking for a bathroom.

The next day our Hungarian guard was on duty. While I and the other women worked, he sat lonely, deep in thought. To even approach one of the guards was strictly forbidden, but suddenly, I was inspired to walk over and sit down next to him. I told him everything that had happened the day before. The guard started to cry as he told me some of his life story. He was a wonderful man. He procured medicine for four of the girls, and thanks to him those four survived.

Our Hungarian guard was sometimes assigned to duty elsewhere but still visited our barracks almost every day. He also often visited the old lady in the bread store and brought me loaves of bread. This bread I shared with three or four of the other girls.

One day when the air-raid alarm sounded, our Hungarian guard came to us and said that he would rather die with us than with all the other guards in a shelter. We were not allowed in any bunkers and cellars, so we found a place in the ruins where we sat down while the bombs dropped all around us. To comfort us, the guard told us stories from his life. He said that he came from the Hungarian-speaking minority in Yugoslavia near the Hungarian border. He was thirty-five years old and had owned a small farm; he and his wife had three small children. When the Germans occupied Yugoslavia, he was called in and sent to what was called reeducation. From there he was sent to Germany for military training. Because he was considered unreliable—on account of his Yugoslavian citizenship—he was put in an SS uniform and sent to Bremen to guard Hungarian prisoners. He was a kind man and no more a Nazi than we were. ⇒⋅⇒

## Gustav
### November 1944, the Baltic front, Priekule, Latvia

An image that was only in my mind kept recurring. It was in my subconscious, and it worried me. I found solace in the landscape around the center of the image that was not like the nature in which I mostly spent my time. I did not really know what the image should convey. When I looked out about one hundred yards above a field and concentrated my gaze within a few square yards, the image seemed clear: it was of a soldier moving forward, but then shrapnel or gunfire hit him. The soldier lay dead next to his machine gun. The image was disturbing because it was me lying there. I shoved the image into the back of my mind, but often it came back.

Now it was autumn, well into the month of November. The

snow had not yet fallen, but the sky was overcast. A few hours after sunset, the darkness was complete. Suddenly, the sky seemed to explode above me. The sound intensified rapidly, and I threw myself reflexively to the ground. Everything happened at lightning speed. Shrapnel whirled around and hit objects around me. Branches and twigs were broken off in the woods all around. The maelstrom ended as quickly as it started, and a thought flashed through my head: "That shell was supposed to kill me."

But I had reacted quickly enough to the initial explosion, and I screamed, "Not you! This time you didn't get me either!"

The artillery attack was a total surprise, and I could not help but wonder afterwards how the Russians had managed such a surprise attack. I do not know what happened in my subconscious, but the image in my mind was blown away. The shell that was supposed to take my life instead got rid of what had plagued me; it erased the strange image that had created so much anxiety. ✼

## Gustav

### December 1944, the Baltic front, Priekule, Latvia

The winter was approaching. Hoarfrost stuck in the trees and shrubs. The fields were thin and white. Before the frost came, rain fell continually for three weeks. As a shield from the rain we had a sixth of a tent cover, which functioned also as a raincoat. My wool uniform was damp but not so much that it bothered me. It was difficult to observe any hygienic practices, though we kept a required daily regimen of toothbrushing and shaving every morning.

One morning an elderly couple strolled by our positions on the front lines outside a village whose name was unknown to me. The houses in the village were far from one another, and in the middle of the village was a church; the elderly couple appeared to be going away from it. We could not talk to them, and so they wandered as they pleased. I deduced also that they wanted to see how things stood with their village. When they got close enough, we made eye contact and nodded and smiled at each other. The old woman and old man walked close to each other and out onto a plowed field where there were some piles of rotten potato vines left over from the harvest.

I do not know why, but something about that pile held my interest. Now and then, I would peek curiously out over the rim of my foxhole and toward the pile of vines. Then one day, when I thought the situation was calm enough, I jumped out of my dug-in position and went to the nearest pile. Underneath the vines were blankets, and I was both surprised and somehow ashamed when I realized that the blankets formed the lid of a buried barrel of meat.

The farmer, perhaps the same man who had passed by with his wife, had had to slaughter all the animals before he left his farm. He had put the meat in the barrel and camouflaged it all with potato vines. He had certainly kept the meat to eat with his family if and when he returned to the shattered village. I wondered what life would look like for the villagers after we left our positions and they returned to the remains of their homes. What would they know? They were completely innocent but had been affected by this devastating destruction. The meat in the barrel was all that they had saved, and now it could also be destroyed.

I put the vines back in place but took a blanket with me, which I would use to cover the wall of our machine-gun nest to keep the weapon clean. Taking the blanket was also a nod to the farmer to the effect that I had discovered the meat but had neither taken any nor destroyed it. I was on the brink of a moral decision—should I betray his secret and confiscate what he had hidden for his family's benefit, or leave the matter alone? I chose the latter. Whether my decision saved the farmer's stash I do not know, but the event is deeply rooted in me, and I think my soul was saved from being

*Gustav and other elite troops were driven by truck to critical sections of the front, where they fought off enemy attacks.*

corrupted. That choice I made was one of the first conscious moral stands I had ever taken in my life. ⟩⟨

## Gustav

### December 1944, the Baltic front, Priekule, Latvia

Days passed in monotonous waiting. Weeks became months, and we experienced both cold and snow. We dug our positions and built bunkers. Wounded soldiers recovered and returned. Others were wounded or killed during sporadic Russian forays. By now, the company was reduced from 140 to twenty soldiers and two NCOs, one serving as company commander. Nonetheless, we were still a strong and quality unit. We were detached from the battalion to be part of a regimental reserve and moved from place to place, depending on the regroupings that the senior officers were constantly forced to implement.

Each time we were moved, we'd spend at least a day in the rear. Nights were used to move us back to the front ranks. We were expected to be fairly rested in order to turn back enemy attacks and mount counterattacks. Trucks usually took us when we were sent all the way to the front lines. Sometimes the trucks stopped only a couple hundred yards behind the foremost positions.

Our entire small company, with arms and other equipment, would be packed together in a truck and then driven at full speed through the night, the vehicle lurching wildly over and into the ruts in the road. We held on as best we could, but we were still thrown about and into each other. Many harsh words and much profanity passed over the lips of the tense and exhausted soldiers. It was not meant to be offensive, and it did ease tense feelings.

We were given a different task each time. Sometimes we had to attack at the front line, other times we were ordered to protect other soldiers who were attacking, and other times we were just sent to other platoons as moral support. ⇒⋲

## *Gustav*

### December 1944, the Baltic front, Priekule, Latvia

Finally, the long-awaited big Russian attack began. Our infantry on the front line had been exposed to preparatory fire for a couple of hours. In the distance, Russian soldiers appeared in long lines marching toward the German lines. Usually the Russians surged easily through the first line of relatively weak German defenses, which consisted of infantry. They performed more like an alarm system than defense. Sometimes a few well-placed and brave infantrymen provided a lot of resistance and managed to delay the Russians' advance. If they did it well, the Germans could get reinforcements and thwart the attack.

This time nothing went well for us who were on the receiving end of the Russian attack. They streamed forward with lots of soldiers and tanks. On the first line, the German infantry hunkered down. Many were killed, and others retreated. To provide opposition to the Russian attack, we had placed my machine gun a couple of hundred yards behind the first line. The machine-gun nest consisted of a corporal, another private, and me. Our nerves were taut, but we were ready.

When the preparation fire ceased, we knew that the attack had begun. The question was whether the infantry in front of us managed to stop the Russian advance or if they gave way and came flying backward. And would the Russians show up with or without tanks?

Events followed one another quickly. German soldiers from the first line came hurriedly retreating. Several had thrown their weapons away and were fleeing in panic. The corporal shouted to us, "Now, they will be coming!" We looked nervously towards the places from which the Germans had retreated. More Germans might be coming, and so the corporal delayed his orders to shoot. Russian tanks, not Russian soldiers, came next. They were followed by long lines of soldiers. The two of us privates behind the machine gun were seized with terror and would instinctively have fled. But the corporal reassured us: "Wait a little longer. Wait until they get closer. Now shoot!"

All the Russian soldiers accompanying the tanks disappeared. Some took cover behind the tanks, but they had no weapons sufficient to defend themselves against my machine gun. The tank drivers didn't know what to do. To move forward without the support of their infantry was useless. How much opposition would they encounter? And did the Germans have tanks in ambush? Was it just one machine-gun nest or were there more? And where were the machine-gun shooters that had just opened fire?

New Russian infantry came up in the shelter of the tanks, and all began to slowly move forward. Our corporal waited as long as he could to give new orders to fire. Firing would reveal where we were and how many machine guns we had. In the end, there was no choice.

*Camouflaged Waffen-SS soldiers in
Latvia, winter 1944–45.*

We had to give up the position before an overpowering attacker. But first we shot a relatively long range shot against the Russians. We stopped them briefly and confused them enough that they could not organize themselves to shoot at us before we had time to escape. We ran toward the company commander's bunker. There we joined with other soldiers and officers who had been driven from their positions and were successful in reaching the bunker alive. ❧

## *Gustav*

### December 1944, the Baltic front, Priekule, Latvia

I had just been awakened to take over the watch. Sleep persisted in my body. It was 11:30 at night, and the long grass on the frozen ground was wilted and covered with hoarfrost. I felt ornery in the chilly air. High above, the sky twinkled, and in front of my machine-gun muzzle was a vast plain dotted with fir trees.

I peered into the darkness to discover anything disturbing out there. With one hand I made sure that the hand grenades were easily accessible, that my machine gun was positioned correctly, and that the holster for my pistol was in the right place. With one hand I stroked my hair back and undid the helmet under my chin. Finally I oriented myself to the rest of my unit. Thus everything was arranged, and I was ready for my nightly duty.

Time seemed to sail away. My thoughts wandered. In my imagination, I saw Russian soldiers standing guard and looking out just as I was doing. What were their daily lives like? Probably not so different from my days in the German infantry. At nighttime, calm rested over the front. Soldiers lay at varying distances in parallel rows—mile after mile. Everyone guarded his section of the front with strained senses, prepared to defend his life. Somewhere in the night a battle between a reconnaissance patrol and soldiers in their positions was taking place. Some were surprised in their positions and shot to death; others were overcome by the quiet night and lay sleeping over their weapons.

Something rustled out there in the dark. I listened, but it was already quiet. I waited a few more seconds. Had the Russian soldiers managed to sneak up on us? Should I let it be known that I was there and fire off a volley toward the place the sound came from? Not to shoot could be interpreted that there were no German soldiers in the middle front section. Then the Russians would come closer and closer. If they knew only that I was in my position, they might believe I hadn't noticed them. If they knew they had been discovered, they would probably pull back.

I aimed the machine gun and pulled off a series of shots that ripped through the stillness of the night. Nothing more happened. Perhaps it was only a field mouse or other small animal that sought food on his nightly walk.

After my salvo, something happened on a hill in the Russian

section of the front. I saw muzzle flashes and heard the clatter of a Russian machine gun. The fire was directed at me, but I heard no hits or strikes around my post. The shooter had probably seen muzzle flashes from my weapon when I shot; he apparently tried to shoot at the spot where he had seen the shots fired. In the dark and without a visible target to aim for, it was difficult to hit anything.

When the Russian stopped shooting, I fired again towards the location of the machine-gun fire, with the same result. The Russian answered my gunfire, and soon we were firing alternately from our respective positions. It was more like a duel than anything meaningful.

After at least four such exchanges, it seemed to me that it was time to put an end to the shooting. The exchange of fire had revealed a certain pattern, so I could fairly accurately calculate when the Russian's volley was coming. And I knew he was outside his dugout position. So I crept up again to my machine gun and fired a few shots but was prepared to take cover at any moment.

On tenterhooks, I waited for the next burst from the Russian that would reveal muzzle flashes. With previous salvos, I had put myself in a protected position but left the machine gun where it was and planned how to rotate it to fire at the enemy. Within a few seconds, I could see the Russian's muzzle flashes. At that very moment, I let loose with my salvo. I watched my brilliant tracer bullets arc from left bottom to right top and probably hit their target in the darkness. What exactly happened in the Russian section of the front is unknown to me, but the firing stopped, and no more shots were heard from there.

The duel was a senseless and foolish prank. With no thought on either side, the spontaneous event became a duel, with a probable tragic end for at least one of the soldiers on the Russian side. ➣·☜

## *Agnes*
### December 1944, Bremen, Germany

The winter cold bit harder and harder. We now worked in a cement factory, producing small concrete bricks used in constructing barracks. The factory was located in Bremen but a long way away from "my street" and "my bread shop" and our Hungarian guard. We received new guards who were much stricter and harder than we were used to.

But once again we were fifty girls who worked together with water, sand, cement, and wooden forms. Four people were assigned to do the cutting of the rebar, and I was lucky to be one of them. My job was to stand at a bench and cut wire rebar into pieces about two yards long. It was not a demanding job. I escaped having to work with the heavy concrete. But it was cold. All the work was performed outdoors, and I froze. Fires were burning in metal drums, and I was allowed to stand next to the fire five minutes of every hour. We stood in line to get to the fire to keep warm for a short time.

Russian POWs did the heaviest work in the cement factory, and thanks to them we got a little more food than before. They received their food at noon, and we ate with them. In addition to our half-liter of thin camp soup in the barracks, we were also given food in the middle of the day that consisted of lots of vegetables, potatoes, a little bacon, and pearl barley.

Among the POWs was a Chinese man. He was very funny, even if we couldn't communicate. Most of the prisoners were emaciated, but he wasn't. I noticed that he often disappeared behind a large compost pile and the remnants of a large greenhouse. The glass was broken, and the place looked devastated. One day I watched him dig in the ground next to it; there was no frost in the ground, the air temperature being about 30° Fahrenheit. There he

*Russian prisoners of war working
in the cement factory in Bremen.*

pulled up fat earthworms and placed them in a steel can. When he'd collected enough, he roasted them over one of the coal fires. These worms were probably fat and rich in protein and saved him from malnourishment, making him stronger than his fellow prisoners. Nevertheless, I never felt tempted to eat cooked worms. ❖

## Gustav

### December 1944, the Baltic front, Priekule, Latvia

The winter nights when the moon was not obscured by clouds were extremely dangerous; the Russians seemed especially fond of the bright nights. That is when they would send small groups into our camp to creep up on us and surprise us with grenades and automatic weapons fire. We could not relax for even one moment. Whenever we heard a cracking twig in the dark, we fired indiscriminately in the direction of the sound. No one wanted to risk the enemy shooting first. We were also concerned that we not be forced to go with the Russians as prisoners of war.

That we were sometimes surprised was not so strange. Once, for example, we were in a swamp that was completely overgrown with bushes right on top of us. Without difficulty, enemy soldiers could come very close to us without our detecting them. The air was constantly pierced by a significant number of projectiles, and one night one of them hit our NCO, who was killed instantly. That left us with only one lower-ranking sergeant. Nonetheless, the battle went on.

My comrades in the trenches changed constantly. On one occasion, a Hungarian joined our group. On his second day, I heard a scream and rushed out, ready to face the Russians on the edge of the foxhole. However, it was merely a Russian bullet that had struck the Hungarian's hand. He had to hurry to the first-aid station before it became light enough for the Russians to see him. Before he left, he told me that he had had a premonition that he would be wounded. At night he dreamed of his mother and a nurse. "And look how lucky I am this time. Last time my wounds were to the little finger and ring finger, and my middle finger was broken, but I was sent back to the front because my trigger finger was still intact. Now that I can no longer pull a trigger, I am finished at the front!" Happy despite his seriously injured hand, he hurried away to seek medical assistance.

My position was so badly situated that no one could approach it or leave it during daylight. I did not even once stick my head up over the edge of the foxhole. Our weapons and everything else had to be kept below ground level. Sleeping during the day was the only sensible thing to do under the circumstances. The only time this routine was broken was when the requirements of nature intruded. Obedient to orders, I did not leave the position but would roll over the edge of my foxhole and with one very quick motion, leap across a path and into another trench where I was not disturbed.

The night after my Hungarian comrade was wounded, another soldier came to replace him. He lasted only two days and then purposely shot himself in the foot. The doctor reported him. He was sent to a special hospital and eventually sentenced to five years hard labor. So a new soldier came. He was a Romanian and did not care a whit about guard duty. Hidden below ground level, he sat on a box most of the time. He seemed always to have a loaf of bread in his lap and continually broke off meditative pieces that he slowly chewed.

Thus the war continued, with no end in sight. ❧❧

## Agnes
### Christmas 1944, Bremen, Germany

To our surprise, we were told we'd have three days off for Christmas. Some of the guards were given the same days off. One day, my second cousin Halasz, whom I had recently discovered, told me that she had been given a small Christmas tree by one of the guards. She asked me to visit her in her barracks on Christmas day. We and two other Christian girls in the camp would celebrate Christmas together.

Around 6:00, I sneaked out of my barracks and went over to hers. There, in her room, my cousin had a small Christmas tree with two or three small candles on it. We sat around it and recited the second chapter of Luke. Then we sang "Silent Night" together. It was such a nice devotion and spirit present. All of a sudden, a few Orthodox and Zionist girls rushed cursing into the room. They had heard us singing and called us traitors, saying it was because of people like us that we all were there. We ignored them and told them to go back to their rooms, which they did. We talked for another little while, and then we separated.

I returned to my barracks unnoticed, went to my room, and washed some of my dirty clothes. Then I went to bed as usual. But I was grateful for this Christmas 1944, which was remarkable in view of the fact that I was in a work camp deprived of my freedom.

On Christmas Day, when a comrade and I returned to the kitchen, I met the friendly Hungarian guard, who said, "Come with me," and led me into the guards' room, next to the kitchen. Two other guards (who were just boys) were sitting and eating. Handing me a plate with a large piece of meat, red cabbage, gravy, and potatoes, he said, "Sit down and eat." The other guards looked away, as if they didn't want to see me.

I ignored them. I hadn't eaten food like that since I was home in Keszthely. When I had finished, the Hungarian guard took my plate and returned with another portion, which he said I could take back to the barracks. I shared the food with the four girls present in the room at the time. The following day and on a few other occasions, we were given food when we delivered empty food barrels to the kitchen. On those occasions, the food was given to us by the two guards who had ignored me the first time. They must have experienced a change of heart. Only we who delivered the barrels were given food in this way.

## Gustav
### Christmas 1944, the Baltic front, Priekule, Latvia

Christmas arrived. To our great joy, we learned that we would not have to replace a company at the front until the day after Christmas. That meant we could spend Christmas Eve and Christmas Day some twelve miles toward the rear at an abandoned farmhouse. We were all ordered to take a bath, and some optimistic soldiers attempted to build a sauna in an abandoned chicken coop. They had the will, but shortages of materials resulted in the fire being insufficient to heat the sauna room, and the bath water was cold. But orders were orders: "Take a sauna bath." We shivered, our teeth chattered, and we got goose bumps all over our bodies as we "enjoyed" our Christmas Eve sauna. After the sauna, we all received clean, lice-free underwear. That was our only Christmas present.

After our bath, we put away our weapons. A special room had been converted into an armory, and all of our machine guns and rifles were locked up there. A Christmas Eve dinner was put together in a hush-hush manner. During this time, we were free from duty and regulations, and we rested in the straw-filled partitions in the sleeping quarters and waited for the big celebration.

Individual soldiers found their way to their countrymen and talked about their experiences. New volunteers had arrived recently. They had signed up for the navy but after training received notice that some ships no longer existed and they could choose either to go home or join the Waffen-SS. All except one chose the Waffen-SS. The one who elected to go home ended up in a concentration camp.

An eighteen-year-old newcomer listened intently to all frontline news about the Russians and became more and more frightened. He had been arrested for stealing ration cards and required to choose prison or the navy. He did not want to be an infantry soldier at the front and worried about how he would react to combat.

At last, the door opened to where the festive table was set and decorated. The NCOs had put together some surprisingly elegant decorations and arranged lots of delicious food and drink. The walls were draped with blankets. Small balls of cotton were attached to them, depicting the stars. We sat at the table, and the company commander, who had arrived only a few days earlier, gave a speech. We listened attentively, and then we began to partake of the food and drink.

Gradually, eating gave way to just drinking. A fellow Norwegian asked me to keep him in check as he began to drink. He told me the basest kind of stories, and the drunker he got, the more vile his stories became. But soon he was completely intoxicated, and I could no longer keep track of him. He got as much of my portion of liquor as he wanted, and I gave what I had left to a Romanian soldier. I had long since given up the thought of taking care of my tablemates. For several weeks afterward, my Norwegian colleague was critical of me for not having kept my promise to protect him from himself.

It grew late; we had eaten and drunk, told stories, and sung songs. I wanted to go to bed but thought I would catch a breath of fresh air first.

Out in the yard, one NCO was dancing, to the extent that he could keep his balance. Behind a barn two drunken soldiers were discussing how they would take out an imaginary machine-gun nest in the barn. In their drunken stupors and with wild howls, they stumbled forward and cast their wine bottle "grenades" in front of them as they advanced.

I stood on the hard frozen ground and fanned myself; the cold air was refreshing. Snow had not yet fallen, and the air was about four degrees below zero, Fahrenheit. The moon shone over the landscape, and occasionally a flare would sweep across the sky, lighting it up and then sinking to the earth again as it ceased to burn. I felt discouraged, and a bleak, dark feeling of despair pressed itself onto me. After a while, I began to think maybe it was not so healthy to stand outside and freeze, that it was probably best to go inside and go to bed.

When I entered the structure again, the atmosphere was much calmer than when I had left it, and drunken soldiers slept in each room. The cook wanted to go to another farmhouse, where he normally slept, and begged me to go with him. He had enough sense to realize that he would not survive alone in the cold and darkness. Once outside, however, he abruptly turned around and went back inside. He stumbled and fell, passing out face-down with his nose burrowed into the straw.

It was early Christmas morning 1944 when I climbed into the straw in my bunk, wearing my clean underwear. ⇒⋆⇐

## *Gustav*

### January 1945, the Baltic front, Priekule, Latvia

There were periodic respites from the fighting, and then suddenly, without warning, hostilities would break out. For instance, at 2:00 one morning when I had guard duty, I was not being overly attentive. The night was, as we used to say, "quiet and peaceful." One or two random shots were heard and sometimes a burst of machine-gun fire. On such a quiet night, one could imagine oneself in happier surroundings, and so I struggled against fatigue and the sheer boredom of being awake.

Then a flare erupted into the air, and violent explosions were heard and felt. I crouched down so that only my eyes and steel helmet appeared over the edge of my foxhole. With a tight grip on my machine gun, I checked the ammunition belt to be sure it was in order. I looked to see if my pistol was where it should be. It was. Then I checked to see if hand grenades were within reach. They were. All the sleepiness was now gone, replaced by anticipation and fear.

Automatic weapons fired. Commands were yelled, and I realized that the noise was aimed against the Russian front line. Apparently, our troops had discovered a Russian probe and were intent on driving them back. Then as suddenly as it had started, all the firing stopped. Moments of dead silence ensued, and the immediate danger seemed over for me. But then a huge pillar of gravel and fire erupted on the Russian side as an artillery shell exploded, and I curled up in my foxhole to protect myself from the blast and the heavy firing that came a few seconds later.

Screaming the battle cry, German troops attacked the Russian front line. After another few minutes of heavy firing, silence returned, except for now and then a single burst from a machine gun. As long as the German storm troops were in action, I just sat and listened more than actively tracking the action. In the stillness of the battlefield, I stared out into the darkness of no-man's land. ⇒⇐

## Gustav

**January 1945, the Baltic front, Priekule, Latvia**

We continued our advance after the preliminary attack. We were ten or twelve soldiers, including a lieutenant, who hurried through a mixed deciduous and coniferous forest. We knew that anywhere and any time, events could result in our death. Our nerves were stretched to the limit. The clatter of small arms fire, engine noises, and the rumble of artillery were deafening background music in the ongoing battle.

Suddenly we were outside the protective forest. We stopped in a small glade, perplexed. Should we advance farther into enemy territory or withdraw? Then we heard something crashing through the trees. Like a juggernaut, a Russian tank crashed through the underbrush and into the same clearing in which we found ourselves. We and the Russian tank crew discovered each other simultaneously.

Everything ceased to operate for a moment. I do not know if it took one or ten seconds before an intensely thrilling drama began. Nothing except the tank existed for us anymore. The tank's turret began to swing towards us. Panicky thoughts went through my brain. Our arms were ineffective against the tank's armor. There was no place to seek protection and no time to flee into the woods.

The turret needed only to make a quarter turn left while it was also changing its direction. The tank's machine guns could at any moment be aimed at us and let loose with bursts of fire. My thoughts were jumbled. The lieutenant in the group saw that one of us soldiers, paralyzed with fear, carried a so-called *panzerfaust*; he ripped the weapon from the boy. Quickly, he took the weapon off safety, swung it up on his shoulder, spun around, and fired—all in a single motion.

Everyone, including the crew of the Russian tank, saw what happened. The Russians were working feverishly to get their weapons into firing position. A mere fraction of a second determined who fired first.

I realized then that the tank had also slid slowly toward the enemy. Oh, so slowly! What should come first? Muzzle fire from the tank would have meted out certain death.

The tank rumbled to a stop. Inside was a small bright light, like the flame of a welder, and then came an explosion. The unfinished rotation of the turret left its gun tube pointing into the air.

What had happened? And what should I do? Would the tank start again? If it did, we could not be saved. Perhaps the tank crew would open the hatches, climb out, and surrender.

The lieutenant ordered me and another soldier to approach the tank while the others stood ready with their weapons. We climbed carefully up to the door and opened it. All of the Russian crew were dead.

Reality returned. Shooting, engine noise, and artillery booming everywhere. Shells came whizzing at us and splintered the branches of trees. All around us were the cries of the wounded. We continued forward and drove fleeing Russians in front of us. One after the other, they fell, hit by our weapons' fire. ⊰⊱

# UNDERSTANDING THE ENEMY, 1945

## Gustav

January 1945, the Baltic front, Priekule, Latvia

The fighting in January 1945 took place in extreme cold, biting wind, and driving snow. The snow cover was about seven inches deep. The frozen ground could easily bear the weight of the heaviest tanks. The showdown was between artillery and tanks on both sides. Although they were mechanical entities fighting each other, we infantry soldiers were in their midst, and the hardships were indescribable.

Three soldiers who had been lucky enough to survive their first day in our camp hastened swiftly forward through the forest. Amidst all the noise of combat, a Russian T-34 tank emerged from the forest and rumbled over the snow-covered area in the shadow of the trees. The T-34 opened fire on the three soldiers. One of them was hit and fell on his face in the soft snow. The other two managed to reach the forest and take cover behind trees and rocks. The T-34 stopped, and the crew probably looked around to see if there were more enemies nearby.

The wounded soldier lying in the snow began to call for help. It was biting cold, and his pain was getting worse. His two friends heard his cries but had no means of helping him and still remaining alive. The T-34 stood between life and death. The two soldiers suffered with their wounded friend, but what could they do? The Russians did not seem to want to help the wounded soldier.

Without a word, one of his comrades cast his weapons and other equipment aside and went with a firm and unstoppable stride past the T-34. He reached his wounded comrade. The Russians looked at him, but no one raised a weapon. Neither we, nor the Russian infantry in the vicinity, nor the crew of the T-34 moved. The idling engine of the tank produced a steady rhythm, but no one redirected his weapons. Everyone was silent, fascinated by the resolute friend's fearless intervention. For a few seconds, the world in which they functioned just disappeared. No one wanted to be the first to shoot, and it seemed as if everyone was hoping the two friends would survive. The question was, How long would it take before someone among the Russians came to his senses and shot at the two Germans?

As soon as he reached his wounded buddy, the unarmed friend grabbed the wounded soldier by the shoulders and set him on his feet. Then he lurched to one side in such a manner as to allow him to draw his friend onto his shoulders. With steady steps, he carried the wounded man past the T-34, over a field, and into the forest to their waiting friend. Then the T-34 fired again at the three Germans, but the Russian crew shot high over their fleeing enemies. Was it their way of acknowledging an adversary who had shown unusual courage? We had witnessed a true hero in action. ⊰⊱

## Gustav

### January 1945, the Baltic front, Priekule, Latvia

The January sun sank into the horizon. The air was clear and cold. Sometimes an artillery shell would land in our immediate vicinity. No-man's land was narrow, and we could see the Russians behind their front line at the edge of a forest. Our company commander had his quarters in a peasant's cottage near the front line. Combat activity was sparse. Aircraft performed reconnaissance missions for the respective units with relative ease, and we were able to move between different front sectors, although we were always aware that the Russians had us in sight, and we needed to be careful when moving.

Noticing a Russian reconnaissance plane flying at high altitude, I did not bother to take cover as the plane slid across the sky. Then, without warning, a shell slammed into the earth at my side. I was right next to a cellar entrance and jumped quickly into it. It was a close call, but I had once again avoided injury. If the shooter had had a bit more luck, I would have been wounded or dead.

When I completed my errand at the company headquarters, I turned back towards my position. Occasional shells continued to dribble down in the area around me, but a scream after a shell landed caused me to look back. Another soldier had reached the company headquarters stairway, which faced away from the Russian sector of the front. Normally, this stairway would have been a well-protected place, but the Russians were so close they could lob mortar rounds into it. The mortar shell had exploded right next to the soldier, not more than three feet from the wall.

He screamed again and again for someone to help him. The medic who arrived a minute or so later looked at the wounded soldier from a distance but did not attempt to help him. One leg had been completely blown off, and shrapnel injuries were evident at various points on his body. He was bleeding profusely, and the ground around him was stained red. Gradually the screams subsided, and soon the soldier was dead.

The medic defended his passivity in front of us, claiming that the soldier was clearly mortally wounded and intervening in the situation would only have consumed valuable medical dressings. Compassion had been scoured away long ago. ❯❮

## Gustav

**January 1945, the Baltic front, Priekule, Latvia**

On January 15 the entire regiment was relocated some distance behind the front. A few new soldiers arrived as reinforcements to our company. We also received another NCO—a kind, nice man who didn't pull rank on the rest of us. Terribly tired, I leaned against a bed while cleaning my machine gun. I had almost dozed off before I noticed that the new NCO was watching me. He walked straight over to me, grabbed me by the arm, and led me to a window. He looked me straight in the eyes and said, "Dear friend, you have yellow fever!"

I was told to pack my things and go with the medic to the battalion medical station. While we were walking, I asked the medic how long it would take before I got well again.

"About two months," he answered.

I thought to myself, "Oh, two long, wonderful months!" The thought alone almost made me well.

The medic noticed my reaction and asked if I was happy to be going to a hospital. I told him it would be nice to get away, as I had been on the front line for nearly five months. He thought likewise and said he wished we could trade places.

We went to the first-aid station, where I waited for further transportation. Before the ambulances could move under the cover of darkness, we were given food and a stick with caramel on it. Five patients could fit in each vehicle. We were driven to a transit camp where we were organized according to how sick we were. I had to wait a couple of hours for my next transportation. In the meantime, I was shown into a room with two beds. One had been taken by a soldier from the air force. His uniform lay on the bed, and he came in after a while. He was not thrilled when he saw an infantryman in the other bed.

"Have you been deloused?"

"No," I replied.

"You infantry pigs! There was such a pig here a couple of hours, and of course he left lice behind. You guys just cannot keep yourselves clean!"

I had no answer for him. He clearly did not understand how life worked at the front and that it was not laziness and carelessness that caused our condition. Keeping clean as a soldier is easy when you live in a house and have access to hot showers every day.

Time passed and I wondered if I would have to sleep at the first-aid station. I sat on the bed and looked at the badly maintained room, the sagging bedsprings, and the lumpy wool mattresses. Life was poor and miserable. Then came the order to leave.

At 1:00 the following morning we arrived at the hospital, and I was assigned to a bed in a large bay. Later in the morning, I was examined. A friendly doctor performed a thorough examination. He did not pay any attention to the insignia on my uniform but only looked after my need for treatment. During the first night at the hospital, snow fell heavily. The morning was cold, and a strong wind came in. The snow swirled around, and the air temperature was about 10 degrees below zero, Fahrenheit. Indoors, we were in our warm beds, and they felt good.

Outside the hospital's windows, artillery fired at frequent intervals. Sometimes Russian shells exploded in the area. The battle for Courland raged on.

In my mind I was with my company. I suffered at the thought of what those who were wounded would have to endure on a day like this. I thanked God that I was sick and that the disease was detected at such an opportune time. I was grateful that the NCO had noticed I was sick, for I would not have gone myself to seek medical help. The disease would have so numbed me that I would not have been able to survive any major shock to my body. ⇒⇐

## *Agnes*
### February 1945, Bremen, Germany

One day it rained so terribly that we were allowed to stay inside all day. Our guards were two new SS girls; our male guards had been sent into the war, and girls were sent in their place. Generally, these young women cared little for their duties, even though some of them were very strict and fought to the bitter end. We noticed how differently the guards dealt with the impending end of the war. Some were anxious and strict, whereas others were completely apathetic.

While it rained that day, I sat down beside one of the apathetic guards, who looked very depressed. I asked why she was so sad and how she had ended up with us. She looked completely surprised and then started to cry uncontrollably. After a while, she calmed down enough to talk and took me aside to a corner of the room, where she began to whisper her story while we both cried. The other girls just stared at us, astounded to see us talking together.

*Female SS guards.*

She told me that she had been lured in her early youth into the girls' division of the Hitler Youth movement, a sort of scouting movement for future SS members. She was then fifteen or sixteen years old, from a small town and a large family. After she joined, she ended up at some camp where she participated in diverse duties on a farm. When the boys in Germany were called into military service, the girls were used for administrative work and to assist in the evacuation of the local people. For a while she was stationed at a rest camp for soldiers in the field on leave. There she became pregnant, and at the end of her pregnancy moved home to live with her mother. After the birth, she left the child with her mother and transferred to guard duty at a prison camp for female political prisoners. She was now barely twenty years old and just wanted to die. She said she didn't know where her mother, her sisters, and her son—who was now around two—were. She knew the Russians had captured her home territory near the Polish border.

She said that at the moment when I approached her, she was actually contemplating suicide. I comforted her, saying we were both innocent victims of this terrible war, just on different sides of the fence. For a while, we talked about how neither of us felt like enemies and then discussed what the future might hold for us. She felt that our chances for survival during the forthcoming weeks were small.

Both the female guard and I felt that the twelfth hour would be difficult. But we committed to each other that we would keep fighting and do all we could to stay alive. In a short moment, we had become good friends, just as I had become friends with the Hungarian guard in the other camp.

I learned that there are good people everywhere and that you can talk to most. Our female guards were not fanatics or cruel people either. They were just people who had found themselves in unfortunate circumstances caused by this evil war. I wondered who exactly was responsible for all of this misery. Was it the selfish, the ambitious, and the sinful souls on each side, who usually get away?

I thought then, and since, that even if a few top leaders were punished, nothing they had destroyed could be restored by their deaths. The only thing left for us to do was to learn from what happened and think about all the innocent victims: Jews, Poles, Gypsies, Germans, Russians, or whoever they might be. However, we, the victims of these greedy leaders, could not be revived unless we put our hope in Christ to live. We had to start anew, begin all over, forgive, and love as Christ did. And that is a long and difficult road.

The rain subsided, and the next day we were ordered to leave for work. Along with the female SS guards, we met civilian German refugees. They were fleeing before the advancing Russian soldiers and had fully loaded wagons pulled by horses. We passed lots of cars that had been abandoned in ditches when they broke down or ran out of gas. The vast majority of these desperate people went either on horse carts or drove a car. They were gaunt and exhausted and seemed to move ahead without purpose. It was a pitiful sight to see children crying, sick old men limping, and destitute families moving along without any destination. It resembled scenes in the Keszthely ghetto or the Auschwitz arrival platforms. I suffered with them, though some might think I should have felt happy at their misfortunes. They were Germans, countrymen of those who had murdered my father, my mother, my relatives—in fact, all of my people. Nonetheless, my faith in mercy had given me courage, strength, and tolerance throughout my war experiences. I actually felt compassion for those fleeing Germans. We were, so to speak, in the same boat.

I wanted God to put an end to all our suffering so that we could forgive, reconcile, and create a new, free world. But the road there was unending. ⇒⋅⋐

# Gustav

February 1945, Liepāja, Latvia

With two weeks still remaining on my prescribed rehabilitation time, the doctor received orders to declare healthy as many soldiers as possible from the Nordland Division. He made extra rounds to endeavor to determine who could be declared healthy and fit for combat.

In the hospital, I met another Norwegian, who also suffered from yellow fever, and we became friends. We, of course, did not know why the order was given. We speculated that the Nordland might be used in an operation to break through to Germany or that we might be sent by sea to help in the defense of the fatherland.

Another long journey now began. Mile after mile, we traveled by train through the gloomy landscape, heading for Liepāja, a city in western Latvia on the Baltic Sea. There we saw a few civilians remaining but not many. A Dutchman was in command of our platoon, and when we reached Liepāja, he went inside the station and reported to his superiors. When he returned, we immediately saw that he carried good news. We were to remain in Liepāja a few days and then travel by sea to Germany. This was the best news we had received in a long time, and we rejoiced that the moment finally had come when we would get out of that death trap called Bridgehead Courland. As we saw it, staying there would lead to certain death or captivity in Russia, which probably meant the same thing.

Now we waited to go, and several nights we were ordered to prepare for departure, but each time we lined up at the docks, we were told to return to the barracks and wait. One afternoon, while walking down to the ship, we passed a few soldiers unloading dead German soldiers from a truck. This was inside the city and the bodies were taken through a gate, probably to a cemetery on the other side of the fence.

From what we could see, the bodies were all without shoes. By now we had seen so many dead bodies that we were generally unfeeling; however, somehow it appeared horrible to see them barefoot in the snow. Certainly they were dead, but it appeared so atrocious to see naked, thin, white legs, poking out below the pant legs in the winter cold. I suppose the reason their legs and feet were naked made sense in the logic of war where sentimental feelings have no place. Shoes and socks could continue to warm the feet of other soldiers, and it made sense to remove the boots from the fallen soldiers, rather than to let the living go without.

A young Romanian about eighteen years old silently watched the unloading of the bodies for a long time, and suddenly a few phrases from the German propaganda worked their way through his mind and out of his mouth. He looked up into the sky and yelled out with great sarcasm, "Happy people, who have been allowed to fight for 'our great Fatherland!'"

He shook his head frantically and with great despair and tears in his eyes walked away. We followed him silently. ⇒·⇐

## *Gustav*
### February 1945, Stettin, Germany

The day when we finally arrived in Germany, we were ordered to march to the railway station to go to the eastern front. The train traveled at a rapid clip, and I was overcome by a deep melancholy when I thought that I was now on my way back. The route taken by the train would probably be the route of retreat in a few weeks'

*The entire III SS Panzer army, of which Nordland was a division, was transported to East Germany and after being refitted was ordered to defend Pommern, at that time a part of Germany but now part of Poland (Tieke, 146–47).*

time. In our minds, retreat was the only thing possible. We had been through so many retreats that we could hardly imagine successful attacks.

The train took us to Neugard, east of Stettin. The arrival of SS soldiers gave the local people new hope. The Russian advance had actually been driven back a few miles. We suspected that the success was only temporary, but for the demoralized town it was good news, gratefully received, and magnified beyond its real importance.

For several days, our company marched to and fro. For about a week we stayed in a large school. Every morning we received new orders, most likely just to keep us busy. It was said that a new regiment of twenty thousand soldiers would be formed there. In the middle of the week, a group of firefighters arrived at the school, and a powerful antitank gun was set up in the yard. The command and its officers were intensely preoccupied with organizing all the soldiers.

Since I had hardly recovered from yellow fever, I was ordered to be part of Headquarters Company. It was a good decision for me; I would have mostly administrative duties, away from the front lines. How lucky for me.

During the week at the school the sun came out and melted the snow. We could feel spring coming.

Suddenly, we were ordered to march. The column was long but missing many of the twenty thousand men it was supposed to have. Perhaps our military leaders thought they could deceive the enemy by spreading us out and then we would attack as a regiment.

The ground was wet and unpleasant to walk on. We marched and marched. The road was soon occupied by more and more soldiers. Altogether we were a few hundred men, unarmed, badly dressed, and generally without personal hygienic gear. Three young lieutenants took command of us. No one knew where we were headed. Were we on the way to Russian captivity? One hour passed as we moved in one direction, and then we were ordered to march in another.

During the night and without warning, we heard two Russian tanks close behind us. Their motors whined, shots rang out, and we heard machine-gun fire.

At daybreak, the roads became flooded with fleeing civilians, mostly elderly farmers, women, and children traveling by horse or on foot. They had left their homes and were fleeing from the oncoming Russians. With the sun, Russian aircraft arrived and dropped cluster bombs. As soon as we heard the familiar hissing sound of incoming bombs we soldiers threw ourselves spontaneously and without a word of command down into the nearest ditch or ran into the protective forests. But the untrained civilians remained in their carts and were unprotected, and the effects of the bombing were gruesome. Only one soldier was killed.

All of this had become almost daily routine for us. But to see small children cut to shreds with bomb splinters protruding from their bodies, women in bloody clothes, and horses dying in pools of their own blood was horrifying. People stood in the ruins of their burned-out homes, their clothing in rags. People and animals ran around in panic. Everywhere were shattered carts, dead animals, screaming children, and the anguished cries of parents. Yet the Russian aircraft continued to drop their bombs over vulnerable people who ran terrified in all directions.

*A farm used by Waffen-SS staff is hit by Russian artillery fire.*

My feelings had long since been dulled at the sight of maimed and dead soldiers, but to see a bloodied child crying over his dead mother was a heart-wrenching experience. The injured child, the dead mother, the blackened ruins of houses, piercing screams, people and animals in a panic—and the aircraft relentlessly and repeatedly dropping their bombs on the buildings and the people. Destruction, death, and grief without borders were the true face of war. ·÷·

*Agnes*
**March 15, 1945, Bremen, Germany**

A military column arrived with three trucks and five guards, including our Hungarian guards. On the trucks was the food supply from our last camp, which was now in a combat zone and therefore hastily evacuated. The prisoners from that camp were transported to Bergen-Belsen, near Hanover, Germany. In a few days, when the orders came and a train become available, we were to move to that place as well. In Bergen-Belsen, we would meet with those who remained of our friends from our last camp. During the wait we decided to consume some of the food that was available. The five guards had a large supply of food with them, and there were only 150 women left in our camp. We cooked soup of dried vegetables, beans, cabbage, and smoked bacon. In addition, there was milk, bread, and butter. We were able to eat as much as we could during the waiting period. We also had smoked pork and flour to make bread. I worked in the kitchen. Our task was to cook and make sure nothing was lost or wasted. We recovered a lot of our strength during those two weeks before our departure.

The idea was that we would take part of the food supply to Bergen-Belsen, as not many provisions were left there. To complete the task, each prisoner sewed a bag from part of a blanket. When the bag was ready, each received a couple of loaves of bread, a large smoked sausage, a package of margarine, and carrots or turnips. Our Hungarian guard believed that the Allies would occupy our camp at any time, and we would find ourselves safe and sound and be spared the trip to Bergen-Belsen. We earnestly hoped that he was right.

At this stage of the war, there were no longer any regulations or lineups in the camp, and we moved around freely. In a grove behind the camp, we picked violets and sunbathed, enjoyed the birds singing, and savored the fresh country air. The old men didn't come to the shop anymore, either, and all work had been cancelled. We found ourselves in a remarkable interlude, waiting for who knew what. Each of us had ample opportunity to reflect on the effects of our unspoken tragedies. ➤➤

## Gustav

**March 1945, outside Stettin, Germany**

We learned that we were near Altdam, a suburb of Stettin, and were ordered to defend a position close to a pump house. Before we had the chance to position ourselves, mortars began to rain shells upon us, and Russian infantry opened fire. We understood our difficult situation immediately: we were trapped. Our commander, who had just been promoted, did not know what orders to give. Our weapons had no effect against the Russians, who were protected behind a wall of earth and had a good view with which to shoot at us. We knew that a field gun could be brought in behind the wall of earth at any time and could then fire directly at our pump house and we would be killed.

A few hundred yards to our rear was a road with bushes and ditches on both sides. From there, with visibility across a wide area, we could observe the Russians should they decide to advance. We could defend ourselves there. We, the rank-and-file soldiers, took matters into our own hands. We ignored the orders of the company commander and simply took off for a more secure position. After about fifty yards we ran into a carpet of mortar fire. It had probably been calculated to hit the pump house but had been fired a bit too far. Luckily, the ground was very wet; otherwise we would not have survived. When the shells landed, they burrowed so deep into the mud that when they exploded, the shrapnel went straight up into the air rather than fanning out. None of us was injured.

Everything seemed to go well. When I was only four to five yards away from the protective bushes, I was lifted forcefully into the air. My body tumbled head over heels as I fell to the ground, with my nose ending up in loose and wet dirt. For a few seconds, I lay still. "This is the end!" I thought.

After a few long moments, I began to think more clearly and to take cognizance of my surroundings. Retreating German soldiers ran past me. One shouted to the others not to worry about me. It was every man for himself.

I realized that I was wounded in the leg and the neck. I tried my feet, and they moved. I turned my head, and nothing prevented movement. My hands were at my sides, and each still held ammunition. I pulled the ammo loads closer to my chin and clawed my way up to my knees and then onto my feet. As soon as I could, I moved behind the bushes and threw the ammunition to a nearby soldier. Now it was necessary for me to get to a first-aid station as soon as possible. When I reached our artillery positions, I rested for a moment and was given provisional first aid. A medic pointed the way to the nearest medical station.

While I painfully hobbled toward the village where the medical station was supposed to be, four Russian aircraft dropped their bombs on the village. One aircraft flew very low and after dropping his bombs turned immediately and took a course headed directly at me. I threw myself down on the ground and prayed to God that I wouldn't take any more hits. My body began to tremble fiercely, and I was afraid that the pilots would see me and maliciously shoot at me. The aircraft flew directly over me but did not fire. After it was gone, I got haltingly to my feet.

It was still a long way to the medical station, and I limped along for an hour or so. My body ached from fatigue, and my steps became increasingly sluggish. In spite of the fact that I had not eaten in more than twenty-four hours, I did not feel hungry. I was entirely alone, and my mood sank. Finally, I reached the deserted and bombed-out village where the medical unit was supposed to be. There was no aid station. Wrong village? I thought for a moment that it would be just as well to lie down and allow life to run out of me. But the will to live is strong, and so I continued my tortured searching. At last, I found an abandoned mill in which a first-aid station had been set up. Two doctors looked at the bullet wound in my leg and put on new, clean bandages.

The mill was only a few yards from the Oder River, and I realized that I had to get across it. The Russians were firing at all the bridges, and it was very risky to try to cross the river via a bridge under artillery bombardment. The doctors and other medical personnel introduced me to a man dressed in civilian clothing who was in the mill. Outside a motorboat was waiting in the water to cross the Oder River to Stettin in about twenty minutes. In addition to me, there were six other wounded soldiers and the man dressed in civilian clothes. He promised all of us a place in the boat. We crept down to the beach and sat in the boat. It took a long time to cross the river, but no one shot at us. When we went ashore on the Stettin side, the five of us who could still walk took a streetcar to the hospital. There we managed to arrange for an ambulance that went down to the harbor and picked up the two wounded men who were lying on stretchers.

I wondered what would have happened if I had not met the civilian in the mill. Or what if I had gone in the wrong direction? Or if I had sat down to rest on my way to the mill and been late for the boat? And the boat? It was the only boat I saw on the river. Had all this not occurred, I would probably have been put into a temporary hospital on the eastern side of the Oder. Almost certainly, I would have ended up as a prisoner of war in Russian captivity, where I probably would have perished.

The hall of the hospital was full of wounded soldiers. They sat, stood, or lay wherever there was space. Despite strenuous efforts to keep the hospital clean, every new soldier dragged in more blood and dirt. The floors were wet and muddy. The waiting room was heated slightly, and groups of nurses and doctors worked among the wounded. Two Red Cross personnel brought in a wounded soldier on a stretcher. There was an empty space in the middle of the floor and it was there they set the stretcher down. The wounded soldier lay quite still but was alive. Everyone in the room saw the soldier, but no one recognized or identified him. Apparently no one else from his unit was in the room.

Suddenly a soldier wearing a white lab coat that concealed his rank came into the room. He bent over the wounded man on the stretcher and fastened an Iron Cross to his tunic. The crisp, clean, red and black colors of silk ribbon contrasted strongly against the worn and dirty gray-green of the

*Gustav received the Iron Cross, class 2, for his bravery at the front.*

uniform. The soldier who decorated the wounded man left as expeditiously as he had entered the room.

Without really knowing how, I knew that the wounded soldier in that moment had died before our eyes, only seconds after the colorful medal was placed on his chest. He was in the same position as when he was brought in but now no longer lived.

His had been a short life. He was young and had hardly started to live, and now his life was over—snuffed out right before our eyes. None of us in the room reacted or even seemed to care. Still, this soldier was a young man who might have been his parents' favorite son or a big brother to his brothers and sisters. He had stood in the center of his parents' hopes and dreams. Now he had stopped living, and future plans were destroyed without a word of protest or the falling of a single tear.

After about an hour, nurses came and carried the decorated, dead soldier away. The space on the floor was gradually filled with other wounded soldiers.

I hardly reacted to the surrealistic scene that had just taken place, but instead my thoughts spun while the hours passed until I could be cared for by doctors and nurses.

❧❧

I had no experience with how it feels to die, but I imagined that those who died on the battlefield died fairly quickly without either physical or emotional pain. I knew from my own experience that being wounded does not mean there will be pain. When I was shot in the leg, it had not been a painful experience, and had I died as a result, I would probably not have suffered much.

Those who are wounded and survive can suffer through indescribable agony and pain after the shock subsides. But I had also seen others who were completely unconcerned and just lay in bed and waited for the wounds to heal.

I had met two soldiers, both of whom had chest wounds from machine-gun fire. The first was deeply affected. He had grown thin and seemed to consist only of skin and bone. Most likely, he had had to wait a long time for medical treatment, and complications had set in. The nurse took a long time to find a place on his body to use a syringe. When she stuck the syringe into him, the wounded soldier screamed loudly, and an unknown substance poured out of the wound in the chest.

I met the second man much later in the spring of 1945. His chest had been punctured in a similar way, but he crept, limped, and ran away from the enemy to reach medical assistance. When I met him he had no pain, and the best part was, he said, "At last, the war is over for me, and now I'm going to the movies!" So there were very different effects in different soldiers with similar wounds.

⇒⇐

Sometimes, but not often, my friends at the front and I had talked about things other than orders, weapons, and the next activity. On one such occasion, a friend spoke of his political plans, including his views on what should happen with the Baltic countries after the war. What inspired him I do not know, but he had argued that the Baltics should be colonized by people from Scandinavia. It was of no importance to him what should happen to the current population.

Slowly, I had begun to question many of the premises of national socialism. I was especially concerned about the principle of Aryan racial superiority and the future of non-Aryan peoples. Who decided that some were better than others? Who decided that some were of lesser worth?

In my mind, I concluded that those who chose these views for themselves considered that they belonged to the superior part of humanity. But what would happen when all the inferior peoples no longer existed? Should the assessment criteria be strengthened from time to time so that new groups suffered the same fate? And where would the final limits be? Should there then be mass suicide? My thoughts were consumed with issues that I lacked the capacity to resolve. And since none of this was an issue at this time, why think such thoughts?

⇒⇐

After two or three hours I was taken to a treatment room where there were at least seven or eight doctors. Numerous tables were lined up, and at each table a doctor and two assistants worked. "Where are you wounded?" they asked. I answered, "In my neck and thigh!" My German vocabulary was limited, but I remembered a word the doctor used the last time I was wounded. On that occasion, one of the wounds was called the *shotstick,* so I used that word, thinking it meant the shot had gone straight through the thigh. However, it soon became evident that I had used the wrong word. When the doctor examined me, he saw that I had an entry wound in my thigh but no exit wound. The bullet remained in my leg. The doctor decided to remove the bullet.

"Lie on your stomach!" One of the assistants mentioned something about washing the wounds. I received some sort of anesthetic and fell into a dream state in which I felt pain and saw how the doctor probed my wound with some kind of instrument. He had a difficult time getting the instrument into the wound; he pushed on it and twisted it over and over. The pain was unbearable. I have a vague memory that I screamed out with all my might and felt like I was lifted into the air above the table. The doctor cleaned the wound, cut away damaged flesh, and found his way to the bullet. With what looked like a pair of pliers, he pulled the bullet out.

"Get down off the table!" All the muscles in my injured leg quivered. The doctor patted and stroked the thigh muscles, and they calmed down. I did not understand how they had treated my wounds. Of course, I understood that the order to climb down from the table was a direct continuation of the physician's orders for me to get up on the table. I was questioned as to why I had characterized the wound as a penetrating shot. I replied that I had a bad German vocabulary and thought that "penetrating shot" meant that the bullet had passed through my thigh.

I was sent to a bed two floors up. The hospital was sparsely furnished but clean and tidy. It had been that way with all the German field hospitals I experienced. This was no exception. ❧

# LAST DAYS OF
# THE WAR, 1945

## Agnes
**April 1, 1945, Bremen, Germany**

One morning we saw a military Jeep approach carrying two high-ranking SS officers. The vehicle stopped in front of the camp, and our guards ran to them with pale faces, and we heard how they were yelled at. We were ordered to line up in the yard and were inspected by the two nasty men, who yelled and cursed at us. As night fell, trucks came, and we had to begin the journey we had hoped to escape.

Our food bags were also taken from us, and the two savages (the SS officers) would not return them. All we got was one piece of bread. Before we left, we ate one final meal, consisting of blood sausage, ersatz coffee, and bread with margarine. Then we boarded the trucks in silence and drove off into the dark. For a few hours we drove along narrow country roads. Then we reached a freight train that was waiting for us in a field. The boxcars were open. They could have been covered with tarpaulin, but not even that luxury was granted us for this trip. The sides of the boxcars were as high as our heads. We were rounded up, and about seventy-five women were ordered into each of the two railcars. There were Russian and Polish prisoners in another freight car; none of them were Jewish.

We got together as best we could on the cold floor of the freight car. The train vibrated and squeaked continually. We dozed and did not understand why we were being sent away in the last minutes of the war. In the morning, the train came into a combat zone, and we saw soldiers on both sides of the rails. They were close to the embankment and fired, shouting and running. German troops were retreating from the Russian Red Army. We were disappointed because we had hoped to be liberated by British or American soldiers and not by the Russians, whom we feared.

At noon our train was hit by grenades. Two of the cars just behind the locomotive caught fire, and then we heard screeching and wailing. The few women who survived the grenade blast in the first carriages, and who could stand, were packed into the other railcars. Only a handful survived, but none of them came to our freight car. Darkness came before we rolled on again. The two burned-out cars were not exchanged. In them lay the corpses of the dead women. To top it all off, a heavy rain began falling on our roofless car. When dawn came, we were frozen and soaked. The sun rose, and we dried off in the increasingly balmy wind.

Around 10:00 in the morning, the train stopped on a sidetrack in Bergen-Belsen. We were told to get off the train and line up. The sick and the weak, meaning the half dead, were told to stay in the cars. We all knew far too well what it meant to be one of them. If a person got to that point, there was no hope for survival, and that insight was now worse, as those left behind understood that they had come so close to surviving. In our car, everyone was relatively healthy, thanks to the two-week break we had received and the extra food we had enjoyed before boarding the train to Bergen-Belsen.

With guards surrounding us, we marched on a path toward a barrier that could be raised and lowered. There the guards behind the barrier took over from those who had guarded us on the train. When we in disordered form passed under the raised barrier, I heard someone shout, "Agnes!" To my great surprise, our Hungarian guard came running over. He told me that the camp was surrounded and would be freed within hours or days. He continued, "Here is a food parcel, so you can take care of yourself for a few days. Watch out, typhus is raging here!" I replied that I had been vaccinated against typhoid fever in Keszthely ghetto the year before.

"Good!" he answered.

"What will happen to you?" I asked.

"I will change into civilian clothes and surrender to U.S. forces as soon as I can."

"God be with you, so you can return to your family," I told him.

"Agnes, do you think I will succeed?" he asked.

"Yes, if you continue to be honest and fair and ask God for help."

We shook hands, and our Hungarian guard disappeared from view. He ran with civilian clothes in his arms to the lowered barrier and jumped over it. I continued further into the fenced camp with the food he had given me in a package under my arm. I do not know what his name was, but I hope and believe that he did succeed with his plan and was reunited with his wife and children. ➤➤

---

*Bergen-Belsen was built in 1940 as a camp for prisoners of war. In April 1943, the Main SS Economic and Administrative Department took over parts of Bergen-Belsen. This entity was responsible for delivering prisoners of war, Jews, and other prisoners to war-related industries. Bergen-Belsen had no gas chambers, but thousands of prisoners died there from other causes ("Andra Världskriget," 162).*

*Agnes*

## April 1945, Bergen-Belsen, Germany

Inside the barracks was a terrible stench from human excrement. In some beds were crowded three or four dead or half-dead skeletons. I had never seen anything like it, not even in Auschwitz. Dante's Inferno must have been a walk in the park compared to the suffering in these barracks. I hung my bundle of food on a nail by a bed and walked out, thinking that I couldn't spend the night there. The forty women who were with me from my transport started to move and stack the bodies of the dead on some selected beds. It was only about 6:00 or 7:00 at night, but the darkness had come quickly, as it does in northern Europe that time of year. Outside, the sky was clear and full of stars. Because of the stench, I attempted to lie down behind the wall outside the barracks, but a guard came and shoved me inside again; he said I wasn't allowed outside. In the distance, I heard shells explode and saw bombs light up the sky. I understood that we were close to or even in the battle zone.

Because I had been forced inside, I went to get my food, but it was gone. Someone had taken it, but who could blame them? We all were starving. But it must have been someone out of the forty who came with me who took it, as the others were too close to death to move.

I sneaked out again. Outside the barracks was a small room about three or four yards square, and there I curled up. There the stench was less, I could breathe, and I escaped the lice, which were feasting on the dead and the dying. I prayed to God to let the end of the war and my personal victory come soon. Again I experienced an overwhelming calm and fell asleep.

At dawn, about ten girls from my group came to me. One of them said, "If we stay here, all of us will die. We must escape! Come with us." I and a girl from Keszthely, who had gone to the university there, went with them. We saw no guards. I told them that the Hungarian guard had said the guards were going to flee. Inspired by those words, we all took courage and started to run. We saw a green grove of trees in the distance, next to a small kitchen garden. We ran in that direction while bullets flew by us in all directions. We reached the garden and from there glimpsed some fine houses and other buildings. We ate turnips that had been left in the ground from the previous fall and other vegetables that had started to emerge, as it was late April.

We counseled together, deciding where to go from there. Then, before we could do anything, we saw an SS officer running towards us at full speed. He stopped in front of us. How was it possible that we were there? Why were we so healthy and strong? I answered that we had arrived only the day before, and all he answered was, "I see!"

He immediately pointed his bayonet at us and said, "Now, walk ahead of me in that direction!" gesturing toward a large, brick building. When we got there, we saw over a hundred prisoners busy emptying the brick warehouse, which was full of military equipment, clothes, white sheepskin furs, shoes, canned food, bread, and other goods. We were told to hurry. Not far away, maybe five hundred yards from the warehouse, we saw a cargo train on a track. The officer yelled, "Load up as fast as you can. Hurry!" I understood the German soldiers were running away with these things.

In the warehouse, we found lots of food. I broke a piece from a loaf of bread and then passed the loaf to the others. I also found a large barrel filled with sauerkraut. We ate with our bare hands; the food was both juicy and nourishing. Then we had to run as fast as we could between the storehouse and the train and back again, carrying first the furs and then the cans. It was extremely hard work; many of us fell by the side of the road because we were so weak. The guards then came and kicked us, and some fired warning shots over our heads. After the third round, I thought I couldn't endure it any longer.

But then I remembered that when I was seven or eight years old, friends and I had played marketplace. We had tied shawls on our heads and balanced toys in bundles on our heads, just like the women in the village did when they carried vegetables to the market. I took a military shirt, wrapped it together with a scarf or cloth, placed about five cans in it, tied it all together in a knot, and ran after the others. The weight felt minimal, and my old game and my motto that you always find a use for everything you learn no doubt saved my life that day.

When one of the guards saw me coming with the bundle on my head, he looked surprised and said, "You really know how to adapt to the very end."

"Yes," I said. Then looking him straight in the eye, I added, "And I intend to make it to the end!"

He didn't say a word, just looked at me, and after I stared him right in the eyes again, he walked off.

When we returned to the warehouse, I suggested to the other ten girls, who were still with me, that we should sneak into another room of the warehouse and hide. When we opened another door, we saw a mountain of white furs, scarves, and gloves, probably knitted by kind Red Cross ladies in various cities, maybe for the soldiers at Stalingrad. At the sight, I wondered how many soldiers would have been spared from freezing to death if they had only received those clothes.

But this was no time to be sentimental, and a few girls and I climbed up into the warm, soft pile, stretched out, and rested our bodies. The other girls got scared and ran back to continue the hard work. I and the two other girls lay there until late that afternoon. Nobody ever looked into the room, and as we heard the commotion settle down outside, we dared to go out. We saw no guards nor any of the other girls we'd been with, only the many dead and dying along the road to the train, which was now gone. We understood that the guards had fled with the train and that the end was near.

The four of us walked toward a nearby military building that we thought was empty, but two armed women in SS uniforms caught sight of us. They started running after us. One of them screamed, "You will not get away!" She was about twenty or twenty-five years of age, tall, and blonde. She would have been quite beautiful had she not had the coldest facial expressions I'd ever seen. We were captured! One SS woman went in front of us and the other behind as we were marched to the men's part of the camp.

Emaciated, naked corpses lay everywhere inside the barbed wire fences. The heads of those who still wore clothes looked like skulls, and I could see the rope that bound the feet of those who had died. Camp staff were pulling the bodies a few hundred yards to a very big, smelly pile of corpses. Beside the large mound was a huge pit, and the bodies were flung into it. Several living corpses were trying to dig new pits, even as they were dying. The SS women gave us shovels so we could help with the digging.

> In April 1945, Bergen-Belsen housed more than forty thousand prisoners ("Andra Världskriget," 162).

Naturally, I was shocked to see all the gaunt, blue-green, stiff, naked bodies with their lifeless accusing and revengeful eyes staring at me. I looked up into the sky and heard myself cry out, "God of Israel, where are you now?"

Then I sank to the ground and remained motionless, staring into the open pit. No one came up to me or said anything, and I didn't move for hours; I was completely numb. I think I was in deep shock. I didn't manage to move until dawn, when a few stronger men in prison clothes, pulling carts with corpses, came up to me and said, "Sister, come with us. We will show you to the healthy women's barracks. You can stay there, because the end is near." I had no idea where the three other girls from the previous day were. My shovel was still by my side. I realized I had not used it.

The men pointed to some barracks only about two hundred yards away and told me to go there. The girls there were lining up for the morning inspection. I sneaked up and joined the group, and someone pulled me into her row. The cruel blonde SS woman from the day before came up to us, counted until she reached fifty, broke the group off, then counted until she reached fifty again. She did that until she had divided us into four or five groups of fifty.

We were required to stand at attention in front of her while she inspected us for a final time. Then she left. Determined to carry out her duties and routines until the very end, she had not the slightest intention of running away. We were allowed to return to our barracks. I heard that the name of the SS woman was Irma. After the war, one of the people accused in the Nuremberg trials was a woman named Irma Grese, who had been the SS camp commander for the female prisoners in Bergen-Belsen. She was sentenced to death for her crimes, and I am almost sure she was that woman. I think that at the end I could still hear her voice shouting, "You will never get away!" ᐳᐸ

---

*Irma Grese was accused of brutal treatment of prisoners, such as beating, kicking, and shooting. She was also accused of having been responsible for selecting prisoners in Auschwitz to be sent to the gas chambers. In 1945, when she was only twenty-one years old, a British military court sentenced her to death by hanging ("Case No. 10").*

*Agnes*

**April 1945, Bergen-Belsen, Germany**

The barracks, a single room with a dirt floor, was packed with people. Everyone huddled together, sitting close to one another with their knees drawn up to their chests. There was no room for me, and the air inside was stuffy.

A young, fair-skinned woman looked at me with her clear blue, kind eyes and pointed towards my neck. She made the Russian Orthodox sign of the cross and invited me to sit beside her. Both she and the person next to her pressed themselves apart, providing just enough room for me to squeeze in between them.

I realized that my brown crucifix was hanging outside my dress. I had found it in the ruins of Bremen and had carried it since on a string around my neck, keeping it inside the thrashed red dress I had worn since Auschwitz. The red dress was the only piece of clothing I had. I couldn't change it for something else, as I had when I found clothes in Bremen, because of the risk of being reported for theft. There was a gigantic Star of David on the back of the dress.

The girl kissed both my cheeks and said, "Njet!" pointing to my back and then at the crucifix. What she meant, I

*Women and children herded together in a hut at Bergen-Belsen concentration camp.*

didn't understand, but she probably saw it as a contradiction that I wore a crucifix and at the same time the Star of David. I don't know how the crucifix had gotten out from behind my dress. Maybe it had happened the night before when I was ordered to dig in the pit of the dead.

The girl then said "Jesus Christ" while pointing to herself and then me. She took out a small, filthy cloth bag, from which she dug out a hard, black piece of bread. She broke it in two, gave me the larger piece, put the other piece back into her dirty bag, and sat on it. I could not have been received into a new group of women with a nicer or more solemn gesture of friendship than that. Starved, I ate the bread greedily while she looked at me and smiled like an angel. She then pulled me towards her and placed my head on her chest so that I could stretch out a little bit. She pointed to my eyes and then shut hers, meaning that I should rest.

I now felt ashamed that I had blurted out the night before, "God of Israel, where are you?" One of His daughters, with the same faith as I, was just like the women who walked with Jesus when He was on the earth. And she showed great love to me.

I was overwhelmed with gratitude that such greatness and nobility survived in the most degraded situation. I felt that the eternal spirit, which exists in all people, could be accessible despite the circumstances. Maybe there was still hope for the world, if some could remain untouched and pure in the midst of all the insanity! I learned that the hope that the world will be a place where all people will love their neighbors as themselves is alive as long as there is one person alive practicing it on the earth. And to this day, it was this unnamed girl who exemplified for me a Christlike life. I felt power and a great calm flow through me once again and knew with a certainty that I had now survived spiritually, come what may. My father's blessing might become a reality physically as well. We slept that night huddled close to each other in a sitting position. ⊰·⊱

*Agnes*

**April 1945, Bergen-Belsen, Germany**

We were ordered to lock the doors of the barracks and stay inside. Nobody was allowed to leave. Panic spread through the barracks. Some Gypsy girls, still wearing their long, fine, multicolored dresses, began to shout and scream hysterically in German, "They are going to drop gas on us! We have heard that they will exterminate us before we are liberated!"

The panic increased, and everyone tried to get out the door; women crawled over and on top of each other in the process. I was blocked in but could still see how they tore into each other to move forward. A few shots were fired outside, and a voice yelled out, "Calm down or you are dead!" Everyone tried to crawl back to a place where each could sit down again. I found myself in a corner. I had lost track of my friend but felt safe leaning against the walls behind me.

We remained behind locked doors without food for several days. The air was horrid, and the time went by slowly. Many had diarrhea, as typhus was rampant; many died during those days. The stench, the heat, the hunger, and the thirst were unbearable.

One evening we heard bullets whistle by; others struck the walls of the barracks. When this happened, I thought, "These are the final bullets that will kill us." Again panic struck, and we all pressed against the door with such force that it opened.

Outside, we saw two ordinary Hungarian soldiers in field uniforms, not German SS. I screamed at them in Hungarian, "What is going on?" The two soldiers, who had thought they were guarding Russian prisoners to be sent to the Allied forces, along with themselves, were stunned.

The soldiers shouted that we had to get back into the barracks, as this was the final line of defense and some crazy German SS were resisting. We could be shot. They then shoved us inside and shut the door.

In the commotion outside, however, I had thrown myself to the ground and pretended I was dead. I just did not want to go back into the barracks. Soon, I understood the Hungarian soldier was right about the danger when bullets flew over my head. I saw the three Hungarian soldiers pressed up against the end of the barracks, taking cover.

When darkness fell, the shooting stopped. I noticed that the soldiers had gone to another barracks, so I got up and started running. I passed many naked and clothed corpses. I came to a large circus-like military tent. Apart from the sound of a few bullets, silence prevailed. I crawled under the outside wall of the tent; inside, it was pitch dark. In pure exhaustion, when I stumbled on something soft, I stayed there. My tired brain thought it was a clothing warehouse similar to the one I had worked in some days before. I immediately fell into a deep sleep.

I was awakened by the light. The sun shone on the canvas wall of the tent. I got up and immediately became aware of the terrible smell of dead and rotting bodies. The softness I had stumbled over the night before and slept on during the night were dead bodies that had made up my soft bed. Strangely, I was neither shocked nor frightened. Instead, a sense of peace and gratitude that I was still alive came over me. I was sorry that those in the tent had died so close to the end of the war. I was now sure that I would survive this horrible ordeal. ⇒⇐

In addition to the mass graves dug by the SS in Bergen-Belsen, British troops found thousands of unburied corpses and at least sixty thousand surviving inmates when they liberated the camp on April 18, 1945. After being liberated, thirteen thousand more people, formerly prisoners, perished from disease and malnutrition ("Bergen-Belsen").

*Agnes*
**April 1945, Bergen-Belsen, Germany**

I came to a part of the camp where I had never been before. There I stumbled upon a young woman with a large, empty water barrel, shouting, "Those who are healthy and strong enough, come with me and help give water to the dying. They are many!"

*British soldiers distribute food to camp inmates.*

Hearkening to her command, I grabbed the other handle of the barrel, and we began walking. She told me that we were going to the abandoned living quarters of the guards, where we could get fresh, clean water from a tap that the Germans hadn't had time to destroy before they left.

We entered the building, found the tap, and filled the barrel with water. The girl was Polish and spoke Yiddish, so I understood her somewhat. She said she had been a prisoner there for three or four years.

When we were almost back to the barracks, which took a long time since we were thin and weak and had to stop often, we saw a large tank surrounded by marching soldiers approaching us. We thought they were Germans fleeing and they would run over us. To our great surprise, the tank stopped, and the soldiers gave us the V sign used by Winston Churchill. Someone asked in English, "How do you do?" Soldiers jumped off the tank, and more came up out of the monster. When he saw us, one of the soldiers cried openly, a second just stared, and the third began taking photos of the surroundings and us. Realizing who the soldiers were, the girl and I embraced, started to cry, and left the barrel, each running our own way and shouting, "We're liberated! We're free!"

I ran right into a British supply column. First came a few tank trucks with fresh water and then a few more with canned food. A fuel truck stopped in front of one of the barracks for male prisoners. It was surrounded by a wooden fence, where the living corpses crowded and begged for water from the inside. The soldiers couldn't let them out, as they would have trampled each other to death, plundered the truck completely, or eaten and drunk themselves to death. The rescuers were doing everything they could to make sure they were saved. I heard the English soldiers converse among each other. They agreed to make a small hole in the fence where they could hand in cups of water to those inside. These English troops were only the first troops. The rest arrived a few hours later during the night.

Soon, without understanding why or how, I found myself with the English boys by a hole in the fence, passing water hand to hand to those inside. Some on the inside drank and fell down dead immediately; others blessed us and sat down to wait to be liberated. The soldiers told them that the next day

*British army vehicles enter Bergen-Belsen concentration camp. The sign warns against typhus.*

they'd get reinforcements and tried to encourage them by saying "You're free! Try to just hang on for a few more hours!" Nobody objected that I helped. The English soldiers only smiled at me.

While we were busy working, a few hundred girls came rushing to the trucks outside the fence and plundered them completely! I recognized a few of the Gypsy girls from my previous barracks. The rest were women who were sufficiently healthy to be able to go to different barracks and to the two trucks that were loaded with canned food. With the canned foodstuffs in their arms, the women spread out over the camp and its surroundings. We couldn't do much more than shout at them to be careful and not eat the food too fast.

From inside the fence, lots of men still begged for water, and we continued to help them as best we could. Once while running from the hole in the fence back to the truck, I stepped on an arm by a ditch. At first I thought I had stepped on a dead man but then heard moaning. I looked down and saw the man looking at me, stirring something inside me to the marrow. I fell down to my knees, lifted his head, and poured a few drops of water into his mouth. He mumbled in Hungarian, "May Abraham, our Father, bless you." I saw that he was close to death and shouted in his ear that we were liberated, to which he nodded and said, "Thank God!" He looked at me and took one last breath. My last favor to him was to close his eyes so he wouldn't have to stare out into nothing like so many other corpses did.

In wet clothes, I continued to alternately walk and run between the tanker and the hole in the fence. Suddenly I thought I heard a voice saying, "Inasmuch as ye have done it unto one of the least of these my brethren, ye have done it unto me" (Matthew 25:40). I looked around to see who had quoted the Bible but saw no one. ⇒⋆⇐

# Gustav

## April 1945, Mecklenberg, Germany

My convalescence at the military hospital was too short as we had to evacuate in the beginning of April.

An ambulance train delivered me and other wounded soldiers to a village with a small hospital in Mecklenburg county. The village was a haven of bucolic peace and quiet, far from the war's noise and chaos. This idyllic existence didn't last long, however. It was not just an attack by the Russians we feared; English and American aircraft flew over the village in the bright nights and fired their weapons at it. We had no weapons with which to defend ourselves. No one knew what would happen.

My wounds continued to bother me and healed quite slowly. Over the bullet hole in my leg was a thick layer of dried yellow pus each time the bandage was changed.

One morning I was awakened by shells exploding around the hospital and inside the hospital courtyard. To my surprise, we were ordered to seek shelter. Artillery shells continued to hiss and explode all around the building.

At noon, the firing ceased, and almost simultaneously the order came to make ourselves ready to go. A two-day truce had been arranged to start at noon so that the wounded and civilians could be removed from the combat zone.

The Red Army was closing in on the town, and we needed to evacuate the village and the hospital to avoid being captured by the Russians. We were compelled to walk because it was not possible to catch a train or find a vehicle. Before marching off, each of us received food for two days plus the address of a hospital in Schwerin.

Two wounded Dutchmen and I tried to walk together to the hospital in Schwerin, which was only three or four miles away. We all had leg wounds, and it seemed good that we were able to support each other during the hike. At night, we took refuge in a small hamlet and slept in the straw in a barn. At dawn, we heard three Russian fighter aircraft. We looked out and saw the aircraft make several low passes along the highway. Each time they dived, they fired their weapons and dropped bombs. We ate a sandwich for breakfast, left the barn, and began to walk the last mile to Schwerin.

Small bomb craters were visible along the way. Severed telephone wires were hanging from broken telephone poles, and we passed many burnt-out vehicles, dead horses, and destroyed wagons. We also saw human corpses that had not yet been covered with blankets. In one place a dead baby lay some ten yards from the road in a field. The child had either been thrown there by an exploding bomb or had run out into the field in panic and been hit by machine-gun fire. We saw devastation and tragedy, and our talking together had long since ceased.

As we approached Schwerin, we turned off the main road onto another street. There we saw bodies of dead concentration camp inmates stacked among other dead persons. A caravan of white trucks and buses made its way through the stream of refugees. I was a bit surprised when I saw that the vehicles came from Sweden and were loaded with former prisoners of war.

All these impressions along the way made us numb.

Suddenly a rumor flew from soldier to soldier, "Hitler is dead!" On a hill surrounded by beech forest, a soldier caught up with us and said that the Americans had already arrived in Schwerin. The two Dutchmen and I wondered what we would do. Our wounds were not healed. We needed medical attention, and if we did not surrender to the Americans, the Russians would capture us. We decided to keep moving toward Schwerin as quickly as we could.

The road divided as it entered a grove of trees. There stood a captain who pointed the way to Lübeck for those who wanted to go that way. We, however, were headed for Schwerin, and so we went the other way. But it was not an easy decision. We wanted above everything in the world not to end up in Russian captivity, but we had no confirmation that the Americans had reached Schwerin. Nonetheless, we put our faith in the rumor and decided to continue on the road that led to Schwerin.

A farmer came towards us, riding bareback on a horse. As loudly as possible, he shouted that the Americans were on their way, shooting at everything and everyone. The farmer became more and more surprised the farther he rode, because no one cared about his warnings. At a curve in the road, we suddenly saw three American soldiers walking toward us. They looked to be a lieutenant and two NCOs, and they were just as excited as the farmer had been. All three had guns in both hands. We shortened our steps and hesitated. How would they react? The three American soldiers had just met their enemies. We knew that they had already seen other unarmed soldiers further up the road. But since we met the three American soldiers in a sharp bend in the road, we did not know how their previous encounters had gone. When they approached us, they shouted that we should throw away our weapons and continue our journey. The way into Schwerin was lined with all sorts of weapons.

Over the town waved Allied flags, and we heard mighty cheers. Some prisoners in a POW camp that had been liberated were out along the roadside trying out the German weapons. We knew that the POWs had experienced atrocities committed by German camp guards. I began to fear that the liberated prisoners would take revenge on anyone who wore a German uniform. Perhaps it would be safer to be inside the barbed wire of a prisoner of war camp than to walk around on our own. But none of the freed prisoners paid any attention to the Waffen-SS uniforms of either the Dutchmen or me.

The three American soldiers were the only ones we met who

were on foot. All the others were driving around in their Jeeps. They did not hesitate to take watches, valuables, and other souvenirs from the German soldiers who were now in U.S. custody. Outside the Schwerin stadium, to which we were directed, several American soldiers frisked all the German soldiers. They took everything of value. I was able to keep my old pocket watch, however, probably because the American soldiers considered it worthless.

The stadium was soon full of incoming German soldiers, who then became prisoners of war. We just stood and felt bewildered. What would happen now? The two Dutchmen and I had forgotten that we had thought we were going to get care for our wounds. One of the Dutchmen suggested that we should show the guard our papers indicating that we had just been released from the hospital and were on our way to obtain additional medical care. Pandemonium resulted when an additional twenty to thirty prisoners tried to do the same thing.

From a window in a nearby house, American officers had a view of the unrest at the camp. One officer rushed to the entrance of the stadium camp to calm things down. The guards explained our situation to the officer, and the two Dutchmen and I were allowed to leave the camp to seek medical attention. So far as I know, we were the only ones allowed out. ⇒⋅⇐

> *The few survivors of Nordland who surrendered to the Russians were sent east; most of them were never seen again. Of the few survivors who reached the Allied lines, nearly all were turned over to their respective countries, where they were prosecuted. Some had to serve prison sentences; others were executed (Tieke, 229).*

# LIBERATION AND CAPTIVITY, 1945

*Agnes*

**May 1945, Bergen-Belsen, Germany**

The first day of our liberation we were given only strong tea with sugar and some cream. The Allied military had brought several large aluminum milk canisters that contained about five gallons each. Someone asked if any of us could speak German or English and could help. They wanted people who were healthy and who possibly had medical training.

I reported for duty right away. About twenty other girls and I were taken in Jeeps to another part of the camp, which looked almost like a regular city. It was here that the German commandant, the guards, and the administrative personnel had lived. There we were interviewed. I said that I spoke Hungarian and German and reported that I'd been given a typhus shot but had not received a required second shot before leaving the ghetto in Keszthely. I also had received some Red Cross education in 1942 and been an active member in the Red Cross from 1942 to 1944. The English doctor who interviewed me responded, "Very good!"

After the brief questioning, we were taken away to be deloused and receive hot baths. By this time, my hair had begun to grow back, and I looked like a young boy with short hair. We were given clean clothes and allowed to rest.

The next day's diet was, in addition to tea with sugar and a little cream, also some crusts of bread. We received four hours of nursing instruction and then began the work of disinfecting our part of the camp, which meant that we put the barracks in order to be burned down.

But first, all the dead had to be gathered and buried, and the sick had to be sent to a military hospital for treatment. The hospital was established in an old military base about half a mile away. It had previously been used by the Germans for recreation, training, and officer education. The German officers had been captured and sent to POW camps. Half of this base functioned as a hospital and the other half as a camp for healthy, liberated Jews until their respective countries or the United States agreed to receive them.

We twenty girls were each given a barracks to work in, together with two to four Red Cross personnel. We were to gather the dead, organize funerals, and also hand out medicines, food, and other necessities. All the captured Hungarian and German soldiers in the area were ordered to dig mass graves. The first day, a funeral service conducted by Jewish, Catholic, and Protestant chaplains was held on behalf of the dead. Afterwards, the soldiers dug a giant mass grave on that spot and placed thousands of bodies into it, after which they threw crushed limestone over the bodies before filling the pit with dirt. This is the location where the great memorials of the dead are today in Bergen-Belsen. There were several mass graves in the same area.

In the barracks where I worked, most of the residents were in relatively good health. We had to observe those who were dying and give them food and medicine. They gave us their names and home towns. The food tasted good and was nutritious. Every day, ambulances ferried sick people to the former recreation facility, which had been turned into a military hospital. As the barracks emptied, they were disinfected and burned to the ground. The English soldiers burned the barracks in batches of four at a time. It was a tragic and surreal sight to see the vast area becoming more and more desolate, silent, and black. At the same time, it was redemptive to leave all that behind once we had waved good-bye.

Afterward I went by military Jeep to New Belsen, which previously had been a military installation. The building itself was of red bricks. The rooms were large, airy, and calcimined white. Each room contained from six to twelve iron beds with a locker for each one. In the middle of the room was a large table with chairs. I lay down and fell asleep at once, and I slept an entire twenty-four-hour day. This was, I think, my body's reaction to fatigue, raw grief, and everything else I had experienced.

The following day, spring was in full bloom, and we devoted ourselves to walking around the camp, resting, and eating. But most of all we slept. I felt terribly weak, feeble, almost apathetic, and totally uncertain about future plans. One morning I felt sick. I had a 104-degree fever. I was placed on a stretcher and taken by ambulance to a large stone building with two floors. There, the Red Cross had set up a hospital under English management with a staff mainly from Belgium and Holland.

Oh, how nice, and indeed wonderful, after a year to be able to lie between clean, white sheets! Despite the fever, diarrhea, and nausea, it was wonderful. I was examined by a young, likeable Belgian doctor who spoke both English and German. His diagnosis was that I had typhoid fever. The doctor said that since I was in relatively good condition, weighing nearly ninety-three pounds, and had received a typhoid vaccine injection a year before, I would likely cope with the disease. I received fever-reducing medicine and was told to drink lots of tea.

After three or maybe four days my condition worsened; I lost my appetite, and the pounds dropped off me. In those days I was almost fever-free in the mornings. I would walk around in the neighboring rooms or shower in the big laundry room. In the evenings my fever returned, and I slept.

When I woke, I felt that something terrible was happening to my body. My heart was pounding so rapidly I felt as though my chest would burst. I was struggling to breathe, and my body felt like it was burning up from inside. In total panic, I screamed as much as I could for help.

The nurses soon came, and I heard one say, "Nerve fever with crisis climax!"

Someone ran to fetch a doctor. In terror, I began to tear off my clothes and threw the sheet off the bed. The doctor came and after observing me said I would receive an injection and I would be fine. "You will get over this calamity," he assured me.

I felt numb and suddenly wanted only to sleep but was afraid to let myself go for fear I might not ever wake up. With all the will I could muster, I cried out, "God, Savior of the Jews, Christ, help me to survive!" Then I fell into a deep sleep.

When I woke up, I felt completely healthy and vigorous. The sick room was strangely altered. I became aware that I was at the so-called wall of the dead. The unconscious and the dying were moved there for better oversight. As I attempted to get out of bed, the Belgian doctor, an English nurse, and two former Hungarian prisoners who were now paramedics hurried toward me. They were amazed that I was still alive. They told me they had concluded the previous evening that I would die in the night because my heart rate was so low.

I had apparently slept for several days, waking only once to cry in a loud voice, "Jesus, Savior and King of the Jews, help me!" I had been without food and drink for all that time, and people were amazed that I could shout and rave with such a loud voice. One of the doctors checked my temperature and found it was just over 98.6 degrees. I also felt hunger pangs and asked for something to eat. The Belgian doctor said, "I am a faithful Catholic, and I believe that God has intervened." I replied, "I am also a faithful Catholic, and I think the same thing." Knowing that we had experienced a miracle, both of us shed a few tears. ⇒⇐

## Gustav

May 1945, Schwerin, Germany

Sometime during the first few days of our captivity the so-called German greeting was banned. The American NCO who told us that added ominously, "If you like the Third Reich and want to die, just stand in front of an American soldier, say 'Sieg Heil,' and raise your arm in the Hitler salute."

At the barracks square and thus also the hospital's courtyard stood the German eagle on a stone pillar. As part of the denazification of Germany, two men threw a noose over the eagle. A sharp jerk tore off the eagle, and it hit the ground with a thud.

Through the barracks windows, we saw how the former prisoners of war made themselves ready for the journey to their home countries. Russians, Poles, Englishmen, and Frenchmen had suffered in German captivity and were freed but surely bore scars both in mind and body.

We did not go outside the barracks, and one week passed after the other. We were certainly better off in the hospital barracks than all those who were left on the sports field. They had not received any food for the first five days and slept all the time in the open air, without protection against rain and cold. The cold in the month of

May was not so bad, but hunger was certainly painful there on the sports ground.

At the end of June, all the patients who were former SS soldiers were sorted out and admitted to a special hospital. As we got well, they sent us from the hospital to a prison camp where soldiers from all German branches were incarcerated. The camp lay in a forest near a small lake. We did not have to lie under the stars because there were several hangars we could sleep in. From the parachutes that remained in the hangars, we attempted to sew sleeping bags. Rations were very scarce, but otherwise we did not have much to complain about.

We thought it would not be difficult to escape. The Americans had raised large tents on the ground outside the forest, from which they guarded the temporary detention center. To jump over the barbed wire and run between the tents was easy compared to all the dangers we had experienced at the front. But the distance to home was too great for us to seriously consider an escape attempt. To wait and see what would happen was a better option.

With large cigars in their mouths, American soldiers went through the camp. Sometimes, they took prisoners with them to help with the work. As payment, the prisoners received extra food rations. A group in our part of the camp was selected for a day's work, which lasted from early morning until late into the dark night. As a reward, one of the American guards took out his pistol and shot a horse while its owner looked on. The prisoners, still debili-tated from hunger, greedily cut pieces of meat from the horse and took the meat in triumph back to camp. Without salt, spices, or any other ingredients, we cooked horse meat for ourselves. Although we cut the meat into very small pieces and boiled it for a long time, it had a rubbery texture. To me, the taste was horrible. ❦

*Agnes*

**May 1945, New Belsen, Germany**

My new comrade, Eva, was only sixteen years old and very beautiful. She told me that her older three sisters and their mother had all died in her arms in Bergen-Belsen. They were from Budapest and had been caught in an SS raid and sent directly to Bergen-Belsen. She clearly had been affected by typhus. Her brain didn't function properly, and she suffered from recurring attacks in which she relived what she had seen and experienced. Sometimes she screamed during these attacks, but usually she just stared with her large eyes and spoke as though she were narrating a movie about her mother's death. Then all of a sudden, she would become herself again and couldn't remember anything she had said or done during the attack. I felt so sorry for her, and she became much attached to me. As I was almost ten years older than she, she called me her new mother.

We received home-cooked food, and after a while we could eat as much as we wanted. One day, Eva and I were going down into the basement together with a medic to measure our weight. We passed a room that was open but reinforced with bars. In the room we saw about ten survivors who had lost their minds through diverse brain injuries. Some were apathetic, some hysterical, and others just rocked back and forth in filthy trousers.

The Belgian doctor who declared that God had healed me had told me later that a room in the hospital held dozens of people who, like me, had experienced severe dehydration during unconsciousness. The result for them was brain damage, which made them more or less crazy. I was so grateful that I wasn't behind those bars. Eva was so horrified by the sight that she told me if she ever became delirious again not to tell the doctor. She was terrified that she might end up in that room.

We went further into the basement and found the room with the scales. Next to the scales was a long row of dead bodies covered with sheets. Two soldiers lifted the sheets and carried away the night's harvest. They noted that only six had died this time. Both Eva and I were so burned out that we did not react.

We put ourselves on the scales. It showed a little over sixty-six pounds apiece, despite the fact that we had been eating fairly well since we left the last camp. I had not previously thought much about my physical condition until I noticed that my breasts had disappeared. But now I was able to walk, and I felt that I was becoming stronger each day.

We were in absolute quarantine, and there were now fewer deaths. Two people in our hall were an elderly Jewish lady from Holland and her granddaughter. The girl was covered with wounds all over her body and lay under only a sheet, moaning deliriously and saying things in Dutch. The older woman was a few beds down and always watched worriedly in the direction of the girl, who could not have been more than twelve or fourteen years old. But it was hard to tell peoples' ages, as some adults in their skeleton-like states were as small as a child.

The elderly Jewish lady had a fine fur coat that she kept wrapped together with some other possessions that she never left unattended. Most of the time, she sat up in bed, but the bundle she kept under her pillow. One of the soldiers said that the two had been hidden in Holland for a long time but that the Germans had found them toward the end of the war and sent them immediately to Bergen-Belsen. He had heard this from the head nurse, who had spoken with the elderly lady, who knew English and seemed well educated.

The girl died one morning before the quarantine was lifted. After they had carried the body of the child out of the room, the older woman refused to eat and became totally apathetic, sleeping most of the time. A few days later, I woke up in the middle of the night to the sounds of two guards fighting over the old woman's fur coat bundle. Finally they settled down, covered her head with the sheet, and left the room. I hardly reacted to this incident; I was simply too tired. The woman and her grand-daughter were the last two who died in our hall.

A few years later, when I read about Anne Frank, I remembered this girl and the older woman. So much of what Anne described fit what I'd heard about those two, even though Anne Frank died in March 1945. ⇒⇐

> *From 1941 to 1945 between thirty thousand and forty thousand persons died at Bergen-Belsen, among them Anne Frank and her sister, Margot ("Andra Världskriget," 162).*

## Agnes
**Mid-June 1945, New Belsen, Germany**

One day, a Polish girl from another room in our building talked with us. She was always so sad. She said she came from a large family of twelve brothers and sisters as well as her father and mother. Most of her family had been killed in Theresienstadt concentration camp. Before the camp there was liberated, the prisoners were sent first to Auschwitz and then via smaller work camps to Bergen-Belsen, just as I had been. She and her twin sister had managed to stay together the entire time. Right before the liberation of Bergen-Belsen, she had fallen seriously ill and was separated from her sister. Now she feared her sister was dead.

Before they were sent to concentration camps, her family had agreed that if they survived, they would go to Israel and be reunited there. Now when she thought she was all alone, she didn't want to live anymore, as she felt it was better that they all died.

We all felt such pity for her. She was barely eighteen, had copper-red curly hair, green eyes, and very pale skin. She looked like a beautiful child as she was less than five feet tall and had stopped growing due to malnourishment and suffering. She began visiting with Eva and me. Eva's attacks were now becoming less frequent and shorter. Together we talked with the girl and comforted her.

During one of her visits, I looked out the window and said, "Either I am seeing a vision, or I see you outside in the street, but you are here!" She rushed to the window and shouted, "Mala!" and then ran out fast as an arrow flies. While I watched through the window, I saw the two girls embrace and understood that she had found her twin sister. Soon, they came up to our room. Both of them were unspeakably happy. Maja, who was our twin, packed her things, said good-bye, and moved to where her sister was staying. They thanked God and me for having brought them together so soon. ═══

> *Theresienstadt concentration camp was a Nazi ghetto established in 1941 by the Gestapo in the city of Terezín, in what is now the Czech Republic ("Andra Världskriget," 398).*

# Gustav
## June 1945, Oldenburg, Germany

Early one morning we were ordered to ready ourselves. A train waited a mile and a half away in a railway stationyard. The road to the train was muddy, and we walked around puddles and flowing rainwater. The American guards yelled at us with loud voices and stern faces to increase the pace, which we did.

Once in Oldenburg we were ordered onto the train platform. We were told to march on our own to a larger area that was surrounded on three sides by the Baltic Sea and on the fourth side by English soldiers. We were apparently being handed over to the British army.

The first two days we were guarded in the temporary camp by naval personnel, but we could move freely about in the area. There were no houses to sleep in, so a large meadow was turned into a giant dormitory, and we tried to make protective tents from parachute material. The food was barely sufficient, and daily we cut stinging nettle leaves and mixed them in the food to increase the nutritional value. The supply of stinging nettles was soon exhausted.

To receive a private's pay, we were told, we were ordered to give our name and regiment. Of course we knew that was a lie; nonetheless, we told them our names and the regiment to which we belonged. All of us who said we belonged to the Waffen-SS were ordered to gather at a farm outside the camp. Except for one SS major, we were all privates.

Once in the village, we were placed inside a barbed wire enclosure on the eastern side of a lake in the forest. There we were prisoners among many other captives. A lieutenant general, a colonel, and the major who came with us occupied a boathouse near the lake shore. Next to the southern wall of the boathouse, I made a bed of leaves and put up branches from bushes to protect the boathouse wall from the rain. The food turned out to be even worse in the new camp and to enhance the food, we again collected and boiled leaves of stinging nettle plants and snails. The disgusting mixture tasted surprisingly good.

Civilians lived just outside the camp, and we tried to exchange the few valuable items we had left for food. The people did not have much to give, either, but one day I and four colleagues managed to trade for a handful of flour each. With the expectation that I would use it to thicken the soup, I stirred my new concoction in a rusty tin can. The soup did not contain much nutrition, but it would at least fill my stomach with something warm. When the soup was cooked, I removed the tin can from the fire but in the process tipped it over. Every drop was spilled into the fire. Never, either before or since, have I been so frustrated by food. I experienced a little self-vindication the next day when I traded a couple of really fine leather boots for enough bread and soup to last three people for two days. The food consisted of a well-cooked snail soup. And the snails tasted really like fat pork.

I do not know after how many days—perhaps five or even ten—but Waffen-SS soldiers began to be carted away on English trucks. I was taken on the motorway toward Hamburg and there entered the former Neuengamme concentration camp. There we were in safe custody, and we had a roof over our heads. The discipline was extremely strict, and for small offenses punishment was quickly imposed—up to a twenty-four-day sentence in a dark cell with bread and water as the sole food. Another punishment was to stand to attention in the sun until one fainted and fell onto the cement blocks that paved the area. With caution, I avoided this rather degrading punishment.

*It is estimated that more than half the 106,000 prisoners died at Neuengamme concentration camp during the war.*

It was worse with the sentries around the camp. They created great concern. Now and then they would fire without warning directly into the camp, and they always hit someone. One or two prisoners died every day, often because of the guards' shootings. Having survived the war and all the atrocities at the front, I certainly did not want to be the victim of the guards' malicious bullets. ⇒⇒

---

*The Neuengamme concentration camp was established in 1938 by the SS near the village of Neuengamme, not far from Hamburg, Germany. It was in operation from 1938 to 1945. By the end of the war, more than half its estimated 106,000 inmates had died ("Andra Världskriget," 322).*

---

*Agnes*

**June 1945, New Belsen, Germany**

It was now mid-June, and the camp was slowly being emptied of people. We heard that the Swedish Red Cross had accepted responsibility for about a thousand former prisoners who had no living relatives or were in need of further treatment at convalescent homes. Soon, they would send more people to Sweden. But it was hard to get approved by the doctors. We thought we had no chance to go to a country that had been spared the horrors of the war. But even if we were approved, the terms said that the treatment and stay would be limited to six months.

Around June 27, the Belgian doctor came to me and said that on the following day, the Swedish delegation would leave for Sweden. He wanted me to go with them, as someone had sent word that there were a few spots left. I said that I wanted to return to Hungary, that I owned a vineyard there, and that I wanted to see if any of my relatives had survived. He reminded me that my home was in the Russian zone and I could not be sure that I would get my vineyard back. The Red Cross could, from Sweden, search and locate any of my surviving family. Then he added, "In Sweden you will get care, and after that you can decide what to do. I don't want you, who survived so miraculously, to go home now into such uncertain circumstances. But we have to hurry! I have to submit the papers to the Swedes within two hours, and I have to invent some disease that we cannot treat here but that they can treat in Sweden!"

I said that I would go if Eva could come with me. "That is fine," he said, and asked me to open my mouth. "You have such huge tonsils in your throat! And how is it with your menstruation?" he asked.

"I haven't had that since the ghetto in Hungary," I answered.

He then wrote out a doctor's certificate for me: "suffered from typhus, has large tonsils, and has disruptions in her menstruation." For Eva he wrote something about some kind of neurosis and that she had to be taken care of by child welfare services, as she was only sixteen years old.

The doctor smiled, saying that we had to get ready right away and would probably leave within a few days. Then he left, and in a brief moment, my future had been determined. ➤⊱

## Agnes
**June 28, 1945, New Belsen, Germany**

The morning of June 28, 1945, Eva and I were to leave for Sweden. This time we headed for the real railroad station in the German town, not the sidetrack where we had arrived three months earlier. When we arrived, all the passengers were in their seats, and the train was waiting for the two of us to arrive. We had numbered seats in a third-class car, and as we sat down, our papers were checked. We also had to state our names, birth dates, and where we came from. The Belgian doctor and two English soldiers waved good-bye to us from the platform as the train pulled out. It was around 8:00 in the morning, and we were heading toward Lübeck, from where we would be sent to our destinations, depending on our health. Before departing from Lübeck, however, Eva and I would rest for a few days while waiting for the Red Cross ship that would take us to Malmö, Sweden.

The trip went through Hamburg with many detours. The track had been bombed, and much had not been repaired. Hamburg itself was a big heap of ruins. The great dome of the station building at the main railroad station hung down like a twisted spider web over the two or three tracks that were in usable condition. Dusk fell, and it was dark when we arrived at the station in Lübeck, where we were met by the Swedish Red Cross. A white bus drove us to an old school in the outskirts of the city. There we were assigned bunk beds in large classrooms in buildings that had survived the war in good condition. I remember we had lovely meatballs and potatoes for supper. A sort of creamed fruit was served

*Swedish Red Cross buses evacuated Scandinavian POWs and concentration camp survivors to ferries and ships in Lübeck, Germany, for transportation to Sweden.*

for dessert, but I could not swallow it—to me it tasted like nasty, slippery soap.

The following morning, we were disinfected in a large military tent that stood in the middle of the schoolyard. We took sauna baths, and some white powder was dusted on our heads. Our hair was growing longer, but we still looked like small boys. Many, who had been ill with typhus, still had bare heads. Most of them thought that their hair would never return. I didn't lose my hair for good, as it had always just been shaved off, and as it grew longer it came in curly. I had large brown spots on my stomach that were caused by the rashes associated with typhus, but they soon faded away. After we were cleaned, we were sent to new buildings where we would stay until the boat arrived that shuttled between Malmö in Sweden and Lübeck in Germany. These days were used to complete all the formalities and paperwork so that the Allies could transfer us into the care of the Swedish Red Cross.

In this confusion, Eva and I were separated. We were placed in different buildings, and I ended up in a room with people I did not know. Shortly afterward, a Swedish soldier came into the room and said that he needed a Hungarian-German interpreter for the Red Cross to assist in questionings and the filling out of personal information forms. I volunteered and went with him. We rode in a military bus down to the harbor. Lübeck was a nice port city with red stone buildings where the merchants' houses, the church, and the inner city were miraculously all unharmed from the bombing.

In the harbor, I saw the Red Cross ship at the dock, but we passed it by and reached a large storehouse. We entered and saw seriously ill people lying on stretchers on the bare floor. Some could barely talk but tried their best to gather strength now that they were liberated and headed for Sweden. Most of them had advanced tuberculosis and were very malnourished.

The Red Cross group was led by a member of the Swedish

nobility, Prince Folke Bernadotte. With him was a high-ranking British officer, because they were also holding a few German SS commandants and camp directors who had been captured when they were on the run. Now they had to be questioned and identified. Most had given false names, but all the information had to be recorded so that their statements could be used in court later on. They were four despicable men who only a few weeks previously were executing cruel orders against their inmates; however, I didn't recognize any of them. Farther on into the storehouse, some of their lesser SS subordinates were held being prisoner, well guarded by English soldiers. There, I did recognize one of the SS soldiers who had been at the office in our camp at Bremen. He recognized me as well, but I just passed him by.

The sick girls on the stretchers were brought forward, and I translated their names and other data. When this information matched with the dispatching sheet from the hospital, the German SS officers were brought to them to see if any of the girls could recognize them. Most in the group of about fifty girls were very sick and seemed not to recognize any of the Germans. The process proceeded quickly and without a word until one of the last girls became as if bewitched, sat up on the stretcher, pointed to one of the four SS

---

*In the spring of 1945, the Swedish Red Cross and the Danish government developed an initiative to save survivors of the concentration camps and transport them to Sweden. At first, it was to be an operation that rescued only Scandinavian citizens out of captivity, but as it developed, the program also involved citizens of other countries. It is estimated that around fifteen thousand refugees were saved. The mission became known for its buses, painted entirely white except for the Red Cross emblem on the side and the top ("Andra Världskriget," 163).*

*Agnes traveled on white buses into the port of Lübeck.*

officers, and screamed that he had been the commanding officer at her camp. Kicking and screaming, she accused him of abusing her and many others. The Swedish Red Cross doctor stepped in and said that the sick woman should not be exposed to such intense emotion and gave her a shot to calm her. She was then carried on board the ship with the last of the Polish women in the group. ⇒⇐

## *Agnes*
### July 8, 1945, Gothenburg, Sweden

By way of Malmö, Sweden, I reached Gothenburg around noon on July 8, my parents' wedding anniversary and also the day we had arrived in Auschwitz. I was in an unfamiliar country without family or friends, and I was with Polish people with whom I could not speak. Nonetheless, I still felt a breath of gratitude for my freedom, my life, and for the totally new experiences that possibly awaited me.

We were sent to a provisional medical station at the harbor for a physical examination. The doctor examining me read in my papers that I needed to have my tonsils removed, but he said I didn't, even though they were large. "We should wait and see" was his opinion. I was then directed to a bus, which had a note on it that said "Quarantine Mölndal."

Before we were allowed on the bus, however, we had to be disinfected again. In a nearby building we gave up all our baggage and clothing. Regretfully, I left my nice suit and nice underwear that I had sewed. All clothing and baggage were piled in a corner and later burned. We showered in hot water and had to wash ourselves with some form of disinfecting liquid. Instead of my dress, I was given a military shirt and a white hospital gown to wear. And I was placed on a stretcher. Ten such stretchers were carried on board the bus, which had room for only ten stretchers placed in

*Agnes was in the top stretcher on the bus to the quarantine hospital in Mölndal, Sweden.*

tiers. I felt healthy but was now lying on a stretcher just under the roof of the bus.

Late in the afternoon we reached Gothenburg, where no houses had been destroyed, and the city was full of healthy people. I felt a little joy and wondered what would happen next.

The bus went to Mölndal, a suburb of Gothenburg. In the middle of the town was a newly built two-story school building, which had a sign on it that read "Folkskola." This school was functioning as a three-week quarantine camp for refugees. Again, there was a physical examination, and then I was assigned to the Hungarian Room, where I shared space with five Hungarian women who had arrived earlier.

The majority of those in the quarantine camp were healthy enough to spend the day out of their beds. However, we were to remain in the schoolyard and not leave the area. I was given a very comfortable bed plus a big stack of Swedish magazines. I did not understand the language, but the pictures were beautiful, and I leafed through the pages, back and forth.

We ate in the basement, where there was a large dining room, kitchen, laboratories, and a patient reception area for the doctors and nurses. We were given good and nutritious food, and I felt as though I was gaining weight every day. But by mid-July, I still weighed only ninety-nine pounds. ❧❧

## Agnes
**July 1945, Mölndal, Sweden**

The days passed by quickly. Since we were in quarantine, we devoted much time to eating, sleeping, and resting. Many days we were outside on the playground sitting in the sun. One day, a Hungarian-Swedish lady visited us. She was in her fifties and looked very elegant in fine clothes and subtle makeup. The woman seemed rich and brought gifts; she gave me a very nice green, flowered dress. Three ladies from the Red Cross also came. They told us we would get new clothes the day before the quarantine was lifted. They promised also that they would take us sightseeing in Gothenburg.

The three weeks' quarantine came to an end, and we received the promised clothes. The dress I got suited me perfectly. I liked the dress and other clothing. For the first time we were allowed to talk to civilians, who came to inspect us. The whole thing felt strange. We stood behind a fence, and people outside the fence looked at us. I felt as though I was on display.

An emergency exit ran from the second floor up through the attic and then directly down to the schoolyard. One day I met a camp consultant there. He was heading in the opposite direction, but he stopped and spoke to me in German. He asked where I was going when the quarantine period was over. I replied that I didn't yet know, and I had made no plans. I told him the future would disclose where I was to be. The doctor told me that he had a nice summer cottage by the sea, where he planned to spend his vacation when our camp was closed. He invited me to come along. He had a good relationship with the authorities, he said, so appropriate decisions could easily be arranged. I asked if his wife and family also wanted to invite me on their holiday. The doctor replied that he was a bachelor. I responded with a resolute "No!"

He appeared surprised. Then he looked me in the eye and said, "You are the prettiest, smartest, and healthiest woman of the whole group, and you deserve better than a life as a refugee." He then tried to pull me close to him, and I answered with a sharp slap to his face. The doctor was very surprised and was for a moment quiet.

I said, "I received similar offers when I was in a German death camp, and always I said no. Do you think that now when I am free I would accept being your victim? Believe me, God will lead me." Then I ran quickly down the emergency exit and joined everyone else in the schoolyard.

We were scheduled to leave two days later. The Red Cross gave ten of us a day as tourists in Gothenburg as a parting gift before we were turned over to the Swedish State Agency for Refugees.

We were stressed but excited as we primped for the trip to Gothenburg. Our nurse found some lipstick and powder for us. We had forgotten that such things existed. After breakfast, we climbed onto the bus that had been ordered for us. The weather was splendid and the mood extremely good as we pulled away. In our pockets, we each had fifteen Swedish crowns, which was our total pocket money after three weeks in Mölndal.

The bus stopped in the center of Gothenburg, and we went straight to the nearest department store. We were not used to seeing so many fine products. Mostly we bought the cosmetics and perfume that we were starving for. Then we went to a beautiful park and on to the harbor, where we stepped onto a sightseeing boat named *Paddan*. On board, a German-speaking guide told us all about the city and its history. We were served food by one of the take-out services from Liseberg, an amusement park in Gothenburg. Everything was like a dream. At 5:00 in the evening, the bus drove us back to the quarantine buildings in Mölndal, where the staff had prepared a lovely dinner. Many of us shed tears during the farewell address by the chief physician. We hugged the staff members and went to bed early. ⚜

## *Agnes*
**July 1945, Loka Brunn, Sweden**

A nurse accompanied us to the Gothenburg Central Station, and we boarded the train like normal people. We had tickets for second class. We were finally on a train as free people among other ordinary free people, yet we had all horrible memories of rail transport in cattle cars. But now we were headed for the spa Loka Brunn, which had a hundred-year history of mud baths and drinking water from the spring. Its golden age had been at the turn of the century, but its houses were well maintained and managed by the Commission for Foreigners. Loka Brunn was a small society itself with many fine houses and a large restaurant building that contained kitchen, dining rooms, and a community room.

I was assigned space in a small house with five rooms. In my room there were already two Hungarian women, whom I did not know. I put away my few belongings and went to the restaurant. To my delight, I met my second cousin and her cousin there. Otherwise, the more than 350 Hungarian women between eighteen and thirty were strangers. All of us had survived Bergen-Belsen and been physically rehabilitated.

I was amazed at the generosity of our hosts in Loka Brunn. On the first day, we were nicely outfitted with clothing. A large room was filled with new clothes so it looked like a well-stocked clothing store. We were invited to try on and choose what we thought suited us: three sets of lingerie, stockings, corsets, two pairs of shoes, a pair of winter boots, and rubber boots. We could also choose two summer dresses and two winter dresses, a winter coat, a hat or cap, a pair of mittens, a sweater, and a scarf. Thus, I had a whole new wardrobe!

It took me two days to select my clothing. I chose a purple two-piece suit, a dark brown summer coat, a dark blue winter coat, a brown skirt with a brown jacket in lightweight wool, two white blouses, a gray shirt, and a wide-brimmed gray felt hat with green leaves. When I finished "shopping," I felt really elegant and reinvigorated. We were told the clothes had been acquired by the foreigners committee from a ladies' shop in Karlstad.

Two weeks after arriving in Loka Brunn, I received a big package from the lady from Gävle I had met on the train from Gothenburg. It contained much knitting yarn and unfinished prints accompanied by spools of embroidery thread. There was also fabric, including some red taffeta. From white, yellow, and orange yarn I knitted a warm, striped turtleneck sweater. I felt happy about my knitting, and the sweater went with the purple and brown suits rather well.

The woman who had occupied the bunk above me in Lübeck arrived in Loka Brunn three days after I did. She was a trained seamstress and sewed two nice dresses and a two-piece suit from the red taffeta. I paid her with my Swedish pocket money. Everyone admired the fine work she had done on the dresses and the suit. They would have looked well in the society of the grand hotel my parents and I had lived in before the war.

Soon I received the task of working in the kitchen. Every now and again, I would sit down at the grand piano in the community room and play Hungarian folk music. Often, women would come from elsewhere in the room and sing along. The kitchen manager's wife, an Estonian, heard me play and begged me to teach her twelve-year-old daughter, who was musically talented. They had had to cancel her music studies when the family fled to Sweden. Although I said I did not play from notes and just played folk songs by ear, the girl's mother insisted and bought a book in Swedish titled *Textbook for Piano Players.*

The girl could read music better than I could, and we started practicing an hour each day. I also taught her "Gypsy notes" with chord numbers. The Estonian student was very talented and had perfect pitch. After a month she played the same Hungarian melodies that I did but even better. In the ghetto in Keszthely I had lost my files of two hundred fifty songs and czardas. Unfortunately, I could play only a tenth of the melodies by heart. ⇒⇐

## *Gustav*

### August 3, 1945, Neuengamme, Germany

Food was in very short supply. As long as we were not forced to work physically, however, it did not matter that much. We just lost weight.

On the morning of August 3, the order came for all Norwegians to prepare to leave. A German prisoner brought the news to everyone but me; only Norwegians were affected, and I was a Swedish citizen. Another German prisoner joined the conversation and said it was obvious that if he could help someone get out of the camp, it was his natural duty to do so. After all, we reasoned, I had joined up in Norway. Thus I was told to go with the Norwegian group.

At noon, two buses with Norwegian drivers pulled into the yard of the POW camp. We had already waited a couple of hours, and so we jumped joyously onto the buses. I was very nervous as we approached the exit gate. After all, I was not on the list that had been called. But my fears were unwarranted. Nothing was checked at the gate. The buses drove through the gates, and the camp was behind us.

There was genuine reason to rejoice. One Norwegian soldier, whom I did not know, said out loud that many had marched to enter the camp. He told us that it had been dark, and they were harassed by the British on the rain-soaked road and could have been run over. Had they run off the road into the bordering woods, they would have been shot to death. And now we were free of our British captors.

The buses drove us to a prison in Lübeck. Inside the yard, prisoners strolled around in a circle. The prison guards were ill-prepared to receive two buses with more prisoners. We were herded into a conference room. Neither we nor the prison authorities knew how long we would remain in the prison. After a while, they managed to come up with mattresses for us, and we put them on the floor. The prison guards stopped and spoke with us in a friendly tone.

When they left, we all went to sleep on the floor using all the mattresses. Minutes later, the door flew open with a bang, and in came three growling people—two Norwegians and a British major. Still half asleep, we stumbled to our feet and lined up. The major looked furious and stared at us. The two Norwegians ran back and forth, screaming at us to stand at attention, particularly obsessed with the detail that our heels be close together.

Under the major's intense stare, we were ordered to take with us what we possessed and follow the three of them out of the large hall. A truck with a canvas covering the bed was parked outside. The guards screamed, kicked, and hit us until we were all crammed inside the canvas-covered back. Despite the frightening and uncertain situation, we could not help but laugh at this absurd state of affairs. For those whose open wounds had not received treatment for several weeks, it was worse. To their pain and uncertainty was added the fact that they were surrounded by loud laughter.

It was a short trip in the back of the truck. When we crawled out, we had reached the harbor in Lübeck. The driver had parked behind a large storage building so we could not be seen from the ship. The British major was replaced by a Norwegian policeman who was flanked by two Norwegian soldiers. Now we were entirely in Norwegian hands. We were then ordered to line up in two rows, a few yards between each man. Then we were ordered to stretch out our hands. We thought that was a rather strange order, but we had learned not to question and did as we were told. The two soldiers checked the wrists of each man, looking for watches. Despite all the plundering we'd been through, one man still had a watch, which they took. We were then judged to have been cleansed from everything we had and were ready to depart. The policeman had done nothing by word or gesture to stop the plundering.

In the harbor we were secreted onboard the lowest deck of a ship with orders not to stick our heads above the hatch. The beds were well made, and all we had to do was just to lie down and rest. I think it was five in the morning when the propellers began to spin. We were on our way out of the land of sorrow.

Because there was still danger from mines, the boat moved only in daylight. When we reached the Øresund, we were allowed to spend an hour on deck for air. There I met four young, wounded men. One of them had brought two civilian suits with him when he left Germany. One of the suits did not fit any of them. For some reason they asked me to try on the suit jacket. It fit me perfectly. "Here are the trousers, too. Keep it all!" they said. So I changed my worn soldier's uniform to a new suit and became a civilian. The four men were completely unknown to me. I didn't see them before or after our journey on the ship. ❧❧

# Gustav

August 1945–January 1946, Grini prison, Norway

Slowly, the Norwegian coast crept up from the sea and came into view. The boat sailed up the Oslo fjord and docked at a pier in Oslo. Before anyone else was allowed to disembark, we soldiers who had chosen the wrong side were to enter the country. We were called up on deck and ordered to leave the boat. The distance from the boat to the waiting police cars was only twenty-five to thirty yards, but at least fifty police officers were stationed shoulder to shoulder, forming two lines all the way from the boat to the police cars.

With clothes hangers or cartons in our hands, we hurried off as fast as we could between the two lines of police officers towards the cars. In the distance we heard dock hands shouting, "Drown the whole bunch in the Aker River at once!" What a reception! Emotionally, I could not take the hatred we met.

As we entered the Grini (now Ilebu) prison about twelve miles northwest of Oslo, we were received by guards who yelled cheerful greetings: "He who comes in here will not be let out for at least five years. Just in time for you traitors!" After a few days, we were informed that the first judgments had already begun to fall. Soldiers who were minors at recruitment were sentenced to one and a half years in prison. The most common were sentences from four to seven years. But many were being sentenced to prison for ten to fifteen years.

Then it was my turn. A guard took me to a brick building. I was taken through a long corridor with cell doors on both sides. At the end of the corridor I was ushered inside the murky cell. This was where everything would be repaid. I fell on the edge of the bench and leaned against the table. Unbelievable and appalling! There were perhaps fifteen long, empty, hopeless years ahead of me. The

*The Grini prison north of Oslo, Norway.*
*The prison's name was changed in 1951.*

guard slammed the cell door, and his footsteps echoed in the hallway as he disappeared.

I lost track of time in the daily routines. I do not know how many days I spent at the Grini prison. The guards called out our names every morning, and we learned who was being released or we were informed about other practical matters.

One day I was asked if I had any acquaintances or relatives in Sweden. I gave the name of my cousin Helge Palm and said that he lived in Långshyttan. Helge and I had spent two months together on our farm in Värmland, Sweden, eleven years earlier. The guards did not explain why they asked, and I did not think to question why they wanted to know if I had any Swedish contacts.

Days later, my name was called, and I was given so-called transport orders. They took me from my cell to a facility that appeared to be a waiting room. Later in the day, with no explanation, I was taken to a car waiting in the prison yard and taken for a short ride into Oslo for questioning. I had no idea what was going on. No one spoke to me the remainder of the day to tell me what to expect.

After dark, a guard took me to some sort of detention center. I was assigned an upper berth in a cell containing four bunk beds. All the beds were occupied. Through a barred window, I could see out into the facility's yard where there were guards and other prisoners. No one said anything in my cell. It was as though everyone just wanted peace and quiet. I was tired because of the day's excitement; however, before I fell asleep, I heard someone shout in an excited and contemptuous voice that a "front fighter" was there with them. He said that in an attempt to incite the others to have a go at me.

I did not do or say anything. A heavy sadness settled over me. Everyone in the place was a criminal of one kind or the other. Yet, they considered themselves worthy to sit in judgment over me. Moreover, they thought they also had the right not only to judge but to carry out immediate punishment. I could do nothing other than to keep quiet, be as comfortable as possible in the bed, and await developments. Sleep soon overwhelmed me, and I don't know what, if anything, happened in the cell.

I was awakened early the next morning. Quickly, I pulled on my clothes and grabbed my few belongings. I was driven to the Oslo central rail station, where a police officer met me. We got on the train together that left for Kongsvinger, Norway, and Charlottenberg, Sweden.

I had not been sentenced by a Norwegian court. Since no one explained to me what was going on, I concluded that I was being deported because I was a Swedish citizen. The train was headed in the direction of Sweden. Later I learned that my sister, Thea, had contacted a lawyer in Oslo, and he was able to negotiate a settlement: due to my Swedish citizenship, I would be exiled from Norway to Sweden for five years. I didn't know anything about that while sitting in the train rolling out of Oslo.

> *Of the Norwegians who had collaborated with or supported the Germans, thirty-five thousand were fined, eighteen thousand were sent to prison, and twenty-five were executed ("Andra Världskriget," 325).*

At the Swedish border, customs officials boarded the train and checked passengers' belongings. They asked to see what I had with me. Everything I owned was in a small margarine carton: two pairs of dirty underwear and half a loaf of bread. The box was held together by a strip of tape about a yard and a half long. It held all of my possessions, except the now-worn-out suit I was wearing. The customs officials were content with a glance at my margarine carton but paid careful attention to my passport. They took a lot of notes. The policeman accompanying me drew his revolver and emphasized that it was loaded.

After the guarding Norwegian policeman and I were well inside Sweden, a Swedish police officer showed up and took me to a police station to be interrogated. Rudely, they asked me all about my life. Another policeman took notes, writing everything down. When they had exhausted their questions, a higher-ranking policeman was called.

"Have you been spying for the Germans?" he asked.

"No."

"There is no sense in lying, trust me. We all know all about you!" The ranking policeman then turned to the others and said, "Throw him into the clink!"

Before I knew it, I was back behind bars. It took me totally by surprise. But I continued to act uninterested and allowed them to do with me as they wanted. It was clear that I did not concern myself with much as I sat on my bunk in my new cell.

I had lost my concept of time. I did not know how much time passed before the policemen who had interrogated me brought a large basket of food. The food came from a boarding house and consisted of meatballs, cabbage, gravy, cranberries, and potatoes. It was food that I usually ate with gusto, but there in my detention cell it stuck sideways in my throat. No matter how hard I tried, I could not get anything to go down. I felt that I would get sick if I ate the food.

I fell into a stupor until evening, when the police came and asked where I intended to go and whom I hoped to visit. I explained my intentions and was told that they would buy a train ticket to Långshyttan in southern Dalarna. In addition, I would receive five Swedish crowns as food allowance. They suggested that I take the night train so as to save the cost of a hotel. That would allow me to arrive in Långshyttan next morning and have time to find my cousin.

They unlocked my jail door. For me, the war was finally over. My first hour of freedom stunned me. With five Swedish crowns in my pocket, a margarine carton bound together by dirty gauze tape, and a train ticket to a place I had never visited, I embarked on my new journey of personal freedom.

I also had some vague hope of getting help from a cousin I had met many years ago but really knew nothing about. Thinly clad, with no overcoat, no hat, no gloves, no scarf, and no cap, I ventured out into the night. The air was 14 degrees Fahrenheit. Everyone I met was well dressed. I had only my box under my arm and the used suit I was wearing. I was freezing and felt empty inside.

After several monotonous minutes, my thoughts cleared, and I began to have questions. The address I had for my cousin Helge was more than ten years old. He might not have remained in Långshyttan, a relatively small town in Dalarna county in central Sweden. If he was there, where would I find him? Was Långshyttan a large or a small place? Was Helge, my cousin, so famous that I could ask anyone where I might find him? My cousin had no idea I was coming.

The policeman who gave me the ticket followed me to the train and into a compartment where I found my seat. With an ironic smile and slight bow, he lifted his hand in a mock salute. "May I wish you a good trip," he said, and left the train. I sat quietly in a corner of the compartment. After a moment, the train started to move, and soon the wheels reached a fixed rhythm against the rail joints. An older traveler tried to start a conversation with me, but I was not so disposed. Only short evasive sentences tumbled from my lips. The train rolled slowly along. Time could not be stopped.

I found out that the train would make a stop at a main railway station along the way. There I should have time to send a telegram to my cousin in the hope that the telegram would reach him before the train arrived at Långshyttan. The telegram cost two of my five Swedish crowns, but I received a confirmatory sense that the money was well spent. Barely had I entered the compartment again than the train started rolling. The velocity of the train and the thumping of the wheels rocked me to sleep. ⇒⋅⋲

# SHAPING A NEW LIFE, 1945–1946

## *Agnes*
**August 1945, Loka Brunn, Sweden**

The radio regularly broadcast Red Cross messages in which the names and whereabouts of refugees were read in alphabetical order. With pen and paper in hand, the women in Loka Brunn would sit glued in front of the radios, listening closely for any word about friends or family members. During one such broadcast I came into the room and heard on the radio: "Dr. Istvan, from Keszthely, returned as a reserve lieutenant from the war and captivity. Arpad and Elizabeth Erdös returned home from the camp Dachau—current residence, Keszthely. Agnes Erdös—present address: Red Cross Sweden; her home is Keszthely."

Everyone around the radios burst into cheers, tears, and screams. Thinking Arpad and Elizabeth were my parents, they threw themselves around my neck and celebrated the news. Of course, they weren't my parents, but I was also overwhelmed because Istvan and Arpad were my father's half brothers. Now I had at least someone to write to in order to ask if any more of the family survived. For my parents, all hope had vanished more than a year before. ✦✦

*Agnes*

**October 1945, Loka Brunn, Sweden**

We received a visit from a Hungarian Protestant clergy-man. His mission was to visit all the Hungarians who had come to Sweden and to hold worship services and counseling sessions with them. The priest gathered us in the community room in Loka Brunn and organized a church service. My second cousin and I agreed to participate—she by playing the organ and singing a solo, and I by singing two Swedish hymns as a member of a choir.

In addition to us Christian women, more than forty Jewish women, plus several of the Loka Brunn staff, attended. After the meeting, we received much praise for our singing of Swedish hymns, and the priest announced that those who wanted to become Christians could sign up with him. He said that the Swedish church's Israel Mission had rented a guest house in Dalarna and that all those of Jewish birth who wished to convert to Christianity were welcome. About a dozen women signed up. Twenty Jewish women from different nursing homes in the country had already traveled to Dalarna, and there was room for twenty more women at the guest house. The priest was hoping to get that number from Loka Brunn. The stay would provide six to eight weeks of rehabili-tation and rest for us who were already Christians. For the others, the stay would focus on preparation for baptism.

I thought the guest house in Dalarna would provide additional rest and leisure time in a more normal environment than Loka Brunn. But my second cousin, who was also a believer—in fact, an almost fanatical Catholic—was furious with me. "How can you live among apostate Protestants for such a long time?"

After I signed up as an already baptized Christian, nine others who wanted to become Christians also enrolled. They said they wanted to forget everything Jewish and avoid exposing their eventual descendants to the same persecution that they and their families had gone through. My friend Sara from Lübeck and the seamstress who had made my taffeta suit were among those who were interested.

Since I was not totally satisfied with Catholicism, I felt happy about the opportunity to study Luther's teachings. Despite my small doubts about Catholicism, I had no doubt whatsoever that Jesus was the promised Messiah. And I thought there should be no conflict in partaking of the holy sacrament in a Protestant church, which my second cousin considered a great sin. I asked her where I could find the Catholics. The Lutherans had sent a priest, and the Jewish community in Stockholm had sent their representatives, but the Catholics were not to be found. Nothing more was said between us about the matter. Not long afterward, those of us who had signed up to go to the Israel Mission for rest and to be taught Lutheranism were told that our journey to Korsnäs in Dalarna would take place in five days.

It was by now late November, and our journey coincided with the first snowfall of the winter. When the train stopped in Falun, it was dark. We got on a bus to Korsnäs, and when we arrived at the Solliden guest house, we were welcomed with a great reception. Imagine my surprise when I saw Eva from Bergen-Belsen! She and I immediately made arrangements to share a room in the small cottage on the farm where she was already living. ⇒⇐

## Agnes
**December 1945, Korsnäs, Sweden**

Christmas was approaching, and we created a play to be performed in a school in Korsnäs. We wrote the script about our journey from concentration camps and, through the auspices of the Red Cross, to the Solliden Guest House in Korsnäs. We included

Hungarian dances and folk music that I had arranged and played on the school piano. We had decided that the proceeds would go to the Red Cross.

At the premiere of our play, the school's auditorium was completely packed. In the audience sat the wife of the colonel of the I-13 regiment in the nearby city of Falun. She was also the leader of the Red Cross there and insisted, after our magnificent success, that we should perform the play again in the regimental gymnasium in Falun. She wanted also to hold a bazaar during the play. Again, all proceeds would go to the Red Cross. To prepare for our performance, the colonel invited me and two other women to her home in Falun. Her desire was simple: "Change nothing in the play. Just repeat the play you performed in Korsnäs."

No sooner said than done. Before Christmas Eve the colonel and I created advertising for the play and publicized the bazaar. The gymnasium was filled to the brim, and the play was once again a huge success. Both before and after the play, crafts and various artful creations were sold at the bazaar. I sold my handiwork that I embroidered from the yarn, thread, and fabric I had received from the lady from Gävle. I kept fifty crowns and gave the rest to the Red Cross. I felt rich. Together with all the pocket money I had saved, I now owned slightly more than one hundred Swedish crowns. After the play, there was also dancing for two hours before we had to return to Solliden at 9:00. Our play and the bazaar brought in more than one thousand crowns to the Red Cross. ⇒⇐

## Gustav

### January 1946, Långshyttan, Sweden

My cousin Helge had received my telegram and gone to the station to meet me. We were both a bit worried that we would not recognize each other. But at the first glance, I met his gaze, and

*The Långshyttan train station where Helge met Gustav after Gustav's transport from Grini prison.*

we instantly knew each other. His biggest concern had been that I would arrive as a shot-to-pieces cripple. When he saw me, he met me without hostility and with open arms. For me things were pretty clear, but I found it a bit surprising that my telegram had reached Långshyttan, that it was delivered, and that Helge was able to take time from work to meet me.

Helge had a rented room, but it was so small there wasn't room in it for us both. He thought I could find room with some other relatives and stay there for a while. When we arrived, we found no one in the lower level of the little house. Helge walked up the stairs, and I crept quietly after him. My cousin spoke softly to someone, wondering if I could stay there a few days.

The family was horrified. A quisling, they assumed, who had served as an SS soldier at the front, would do everything that is bad: smoke, drink, fight, swear, and worse. Then I showed myself at the door on the upper level. The fellow they saw looked very different from the traitor they had imagined. I was pale, skinny, and not very big.

The first night, my cousin Helge and I talked about what we had done with ourselves since we were boys in Värmland. It was pure coincidence that Helge was in Långshyttan and that we had met. Had Helge not been in Långshyttan when I arrived, everything would have been much more difficult for me. How was I to adjust to civilian life? I was so unaccustomed to acting on my own after the time I had spent in the German military, where I simply followed orders, that I felt indifferent, even lethargic, with regard to the decisions I had to make on my own. Sure, I wanted both a job and an apartment, but I could not do anything to make my desires become reality. It was as though I were in a fog.

Luckily, after a few days, Helge received the information he had been waiting for. He had arranged, without my knowledge, for me to take over both his job and his apartment. I began to eat in the cafeteria Lergöken, where Helge had eaten. I did not do anything myself; I just accepted what had transpired. Somehow, it was obvious to me that everything would work out, but I had no ability to pursue any initiative.

At this point I had not yet begun to think about the future. I lived everything apathetically within myself. Slowly, however, after years of being told what to do, I began to normalize. I was now an industrial worker who worked shifts. My department was small—we were only three men—and our job was to get the hot ingots to the mill in the iron works. My shift was mornings starting at 5:30 and ending at 2:00 in the afternoon. That suited me fine since I had time for other things in the afternoon.

The first working day went well, although it was hard work. When I sat down to eat dinner, I noticed that my hands shook and I was weak in the knees. Was I going to get sick now that better times were just starting? I was scared at the thought. No money, no health insurance, and no one to rely on. Pessimism pressed on me. The hope for brighter days that had started to rise within me was rapidly getting darker. But then I realized that I was doing work that was new for me and that I was both weak and untrained. For my hands to shake and my knees to tremble was probably quite normal. After a few minutes, I stopped shaking and trembling. The food began to taste good, and so I was quickly restored. I went early to bed on the first workday evening.

My new life began to take shape, and it seemed rather pleasant. When I finished my day, I could do whatever I wanted, and no one appeared to care. Even if I were to get sick, I didn't think anyone would care. Such was freedom.

After a few days, I noticed that I was being watched by others. At a table in the cafeteria, I overheard a man and a woman talking about me. They spoke in low tones, looking around to influence others. The woman said something that got the man to turn toward me and mockingly say, "Well, he looks like a better kind of bum."

The words stung. I shouldn't have paid any attention to a few idle words, but I couldn't help it. I learned that freedom means not only freedom for me but also freedom for everyone else to do what pleases them. Maybe I had to build up a defense of my freedom, if I wanted to keep it. I had no means to reach out and create a defense. As far as I knew, I had only one defense, and that was not to open myself up more than absolutely necessary.

In the workplace, I was regarded with suspicion. In a place where Swedish was spoken, my speech was mixed with Norwegian words. I said nothing about my past or origins. To avoid controversy or conflict, I kept to myself.

It turned out that I was better known in Långshyttan than I thought. One day when I passed through the factory gate, I was stopped by the guard, who started a conversation with me. It seems that more than twelve years before, he had visited my parents in Värmland and had even met me. I remembered his visit to us; the guard was one of my father's distant relatives. We exchanged a few words, but I was keen not to show too much interest in becoming closer acquaintances. I did not realize the value of knowing people during the period of my transformation.

To my way of thinking, I needed to isolate myself from people—perhaps by taking employment in some unknown and remote place. Deep in Jämtland in northern Sweden could be a suitable place. I realized that the thoughts were just a way to escape my problems. Maybe my dark thoughts were a part of the process of getting through the initial period of freedom. Reintegration into society went on its own. People and authorities intruded, though with most, the intrusion was not intentional or from their side.

Without a doubt, it was difficult to leave the old war life behind. One day I went exploring around the mill to see how it looked. Suddenly, something snapped right next to me, and steam poured out in a cloud just a few feet away. My instinct was to throw myself on the ground to avoid shrapnel that was sure to come. I was already on my knees before I realized my mistake. Quickly, I looked around to see if anyone had observed my reaction. I was alone. I concluded, "There is no war here." I could forget the front-line reflexes. ⇒·⇐

## *Agnes*
### February 1946, Långshyttan, Sweden

I accepted an offer to work in the kitchen at the ironworks in Långshyttan. My plan was to stay in Sweden for at least a year. During that time, I expected to get clear information about my relatives in Hungary. I was hopeful that by then the war wounds would have had time to heal in the rest of Europe. My ticket to

Långshyttan was printed in the ticket booth at the bus station in Falun; on the ticket was the date stamp: 1 February 1946.

The journey to Långshyttan took about three hours and when I got off the bus, my sponsor family's relatives were waiting for me. They had arranged a clean, spacious, and airy room for me, which I shared with a Swedish woman who also worked as a waitress in the business owned by my sponsor family's relatives. I found out that food, laundry, room, and rent amounted to 100 Swedish crowns a month, and that would be my salary, which I understood to be a normal wage for a woman my age. The job as a kitchen helper and waitress in Långshyttan was my first paid job, and it marked also the beginning of a new life for me.  ⇒⇐

## Gustav

### Spring 1946, Långshyttan, Sweden

The spring of 1946, something happened that was not supposed to happen—I got sick. Although it was only a cold, I had to stay in bed. One morning, I experienced nausea and violent vomiting. I was so weak that I did not think of anything. I should have notified my workplace, but I just lay there and felt miserable in the small, poorly maintained room that I shared with one other person. I was twenty-three years old, had only a few clothes and no money, and felt completely ostracized from society. That was a very low time for me.

In the newspapers and on the radio the facts of Nazism began to be revealed. I had heard of some of it before but had always dismissed it as propaganda. For me it was inconceivable that Germany, a great nation of culture and technology, could be behind the horror that I was hearing more and more about. But now it turned out to be true, and I had taken part in all this. I had served in the Waffen-SS in good faith, but no one now wanted to see it

that way. I felt that there was no help and no support there for me.
I felt indescribably uncomfortable.

A memory from our retreat grew in my mind of a little boy and
his dying sister, whom I had seen with their dead mother in northern Germany. The boy, completely at the mercy of war and chaos,
stood next to a bloody pile of trash. What had happened to him?
Had he been run over and killed, or had he met a Good Samaritan?
As I thought about that, my thoughts turned into words, which I
wrote down:

> *In ninety hundred forty-five,*
> *When the war was almost over,*
> *When many abandoned their homes*
> *And aimlessly fled westward,*
> *I saw two children and their mother.*
> *On an early morning dash—*
> *Horse and carriage at full gallop*
> *Among rocks, crevasses, dirt, and dust.*
> *They fled the danger, but to what purpose?*
> *At the sound of a flying machine,*
> *They fled with even greater haste.*
> *But the plane dived towards the road,*
> *And unleashed its horrible cargo*
> *To strike the defenseless refugee stream.*
> *Shrouded in smoke—like a wall.*
> *The family's final tragedy itself*
> *Was inaugurated in a scourge of fire*
> *And the past was past.*
> *Then out of sight the plane disappeared.*
> *I saw only senseless sorrow and distress:*
> *Everything was chaos.*
> *The spirited horse was now dead.*

*And without wheels the carriage lay there.*
*A bloody corpse from the wreckage fell;*
*And the boy his sister held*
*With her stomach ripped open.*
*And terribly he screamed at the death of his mother.*

An hour after I should have been at work, a colleague knocked on my door and stepped inside. When I had not arrived at the start of the shift, he thought I had overslept. So that I would not miss my wages, he had stamped me in and then had run the three hundred yards to my rented room to wake me. When he saw that I was sick, he was vexed. To stamp my card once without being detected was risky. But to stamp it a second time at the end of the shift without it being found out would be next to impossible. And to stamp for each other was strictly forbidden. So that my coworker would not get in trouble, I had no choice—I needed to get up and go to work.

It was fortunate for both of us that my absence had not been noted. In the workplace, I continued to vomit, but with great effort I held out throughout the shift and stamped myself out. No one had to get in trouble, and I was grateful to my colleague for desiring to assist me. When I left work, I did not care about going to the Lergöken cafeteria at the ironworks. I had no appetite and went straight home to bed.

I was completely surprised the next day when a woman who was a total stranger to me stood in the doorway with a tray of food. She looked quickly about the room, turned sharply around, and returned after a few minutes with, as she said, "a more appropriate diet." She was definitely the person who was needed in that situation, but who was she, and why had she come? She came twice before I was well enough to go to the cafeteria after work.

I could hardly come to grips with what had happened. Two

*The Långshyttan ironworks, where Gustav worked.*

people had shown me kindness and friendliness! Did I dare to forsake thoughts of abandonment? Two persons, for reasons completely unknown, had shown interest in me and exhibited compassion and helpfulness far beyond what I could have imagined. Perhaps the future was not as bleak as I had thought. ❧❧

# A LIFE TOGETHER, 1946–1951

## *Agnes*

**March 1946, Långshyttan, Sweden**

The place where meals were served in the Långshyttan iron-works was called Lergöken. Those who were served meals lived in a row of houses in which there were some twenty rooms. Two people lived in each room; most were bachelors who worked at the mill. The boss lady lived in her own room, and I shared a room with a woman named Siri. A small pantry and a gathering hall also belonged to the row houses with rooms.

Siri and I worked two shifts that changed every two weeks. The first week was the shift from 5:00 in the morning until 2:00 in the afternoon. The second week we worked from 2:00 in the afternoon to 11:00 at night. Workers who began their job at the mill at 6:00 in the morning ate breakfast at 5:00 and received a packed lunch for the day. We served lunch from 1:00 in the afternoon until 3:00. Those who started working at the mill at 2:00 had lunch at 1:00. They who ended their work shift at 2:00 in the afternoon ate lunch sometime before 3:00. Those who worked until 10:00 in the evening could not eat dinner until 11:00.

The camaraderie we enjoyed among us was nice. Initially,

*The cafeteria Lergöken outside the steel works in Långshyttan where Agnes had her first job and where Gustav ate every day before or after his shift.*

it was quite challenging, since I did not even know the Swedish words for knife and fork. But with many questions and much laughter, I learned quickly enough of the Swedish language to serve in the dining hall.

In early March, I noticed a young man—so miserable, so lean, and so pale, almost green in his face—standing in the lunchroom queue. He had beautiful, sad, kind eyes and turned out to be half Norwegian. I later learned he was named Gustav.

One day I saw that his seat was empty and his plate untouched. Our supervisor said that Gustav was sick and that he rented a room from a photographer right next to Lergöken. With no ulterior motive, I made ready a tray of pork chops, went to Gustav's room, and knocked.

The photographer's wife opened the door and showed me to Gustav's room. He looked even more pale, and I could see that he really felt bad. He would not be able to tolerate the food on my tray. He vomited. I quickly returned to the restaurant and put together biscuits and tea. While he ate, I cleaned up the room a bit. The next day I did the same thing. On the third day, Gustav was healthy enough to again appear in Lergöken.

When I took the food tray to Gustav, I had noticed the photographer family's nice piano standing in the parlor. I asked the lady if I could play the piano at some point when I was off work. The first time I sat at the piano and played Hungarian folk songs, both the photographer's wife and Gustav suddenly appeared in the doorway and applauded.

Several evenings later, I walked to a bench on the hill near Lergöken. As I sat pondering, Gustav shyly came up behind me and asked if he could invite me to the movies in appreciation for me giving him food when he was sick. "Sure," I replied. Sitting in the dark cinema, Gustav's hand brushed mine. I quickly grabbed his hand and held it throughout the film. And that is how it all began. ⚓

## *Gustav*
### March 1946, Långshyttan, Sweden

Three days later, still in March, I saw the caring young woman sitting on a bench not far from Lergöken. I asked her to the movies as thanks for having been kind and bringing me food when I was sick. With wages in my pocket, I could afford to pay for two cinema tickets at twenty-five öre each (about five cents each). Without hesitation, the young women thanked me and said yes. I did not know her name, and she didn't know mine either.

We told our names to each other and went to the cinema. We began to meet more frequently. We each had little money, but neither of us really missed anything. Our circumstances in life were new for us, and we accepted them. Our long walks and talks—we spoke German with each other—took the place of what we did not have. Until then, I had seen people as individuals in the world, divided into the two sexes, but I had not discovered what impact women could have until then. Agnes meant more and more to me.

I think it was the third time that we went walking when I told her about my background. I expected a violent reaction from her, but she said that she had always understood who I was and what I had been doing during the war. She had imagined it. Deep down, I probably would not have expected any other reaction from Agnes. Everything was so obvious. She later said that she cried that night before she fell asleep. Our relationship only got stronger, and soon there were ties between us that could no longer be broken so easily. ⇒⋅⇐

## *Agnes*
### Summer–Fall 1946, Långshyttan, Sweden

Gustav was twenty-four and I was twenty-seven, and we were truly in love. We needed each other. He was alone and I was alone, but together we had each other. We talked and walked and talked and walked. In the middle of the summer, Gustav moved to work with his father in the forests. The pay was better than in the Långshyttan ironworks; he wanted to save enough money to afford a one-year commercial training course in Katrineholm. Although Gustav came from the forest and visited me in Långshyttan every Sunday, I felt lonely during the week.

The trade school in Katrineholm began in August. Starting in September, Gustav came every weekend to visit me. He stayed with his aunt who lived in Långshyttan. On September 12, we got engaged and planned our wedding for Christmas 1946.

One day I decided to go to Katrineholm to surprise Gustav and say hello to him. The journey took longer than I had imagined it would. When I arrived, I asked where the school was and immediately went there. Gustav did not know I was coming, and I stood just outside the schoolyard waiting for the students to come out on break.

After half an hour, men and women began pouring out of the building. Gustav was in a group of women; I went with decisive steps into his group, lifted my arms, embraced him, and whispered in his ear: "Kiss me." Then I gave Gustav a firm kiss, right in front of all the other women. I wanted them to know that Gustav was mine. He was more than a little surprised and could not bring himself to say anything. I took his hand, and we walked away to a quiet corner in the schoolyard to talk. ⊰⊱

## Gustav

### Fall 1946, Katrineholm, Sweden

On a sunny, beautiful day when all the trade school students were on lunch break, standing outside and enjoying the season, Agnes came into the playground and walked straight through all the students to me. The students followed Agnes with their eyes and looked curiously at us. Everyone knew that she was not a student.

Agnes and I talked for a while. When she was going she suddenly said, in a way that I could not refuse, "Kiss me."

Her body language, voice, and eyes told me that the response to her request was absolutely crucial for her, perhaps for the rest of her life. A no from me would have meant that our relationship was broken. The scene in the schoolyard was witnessed by silent trade school students with all eyes on the two of us. Agnes received her kiss,

*Gustav, 1946.*

and the scene dissolved. We walked a few steps aside, holding each other's hand and talking.

Then Agnes walked in triumph, passing the other students, out of the schoolyard. The self-confidence on her face told any possible competitors, "Stay away! Gustav is mine." This moment was a culmination of her longings and a compensation for all of her tragedies, sorrows, and sufferings. ⨯⨯

## *Agnes*
**Fall 1946–March 2, 1947, Katrineholm, Sweden**

I applied for and received a job in Katrineholm where Gustav ate his lunch during school. I was to begin work there in January 1947. Happy, I took the bus back to Långshyttan. While I was still in Långshyttan, every weekend Gustav stayed with his relatives and we spent all the time we could together. I truly longed for him when he was gone.

The priest in the Swedish church in Långshyttan called us just

before Christmas to tell us that he could not marry us until I got my birth certificate from Hungary. Until then we thought everything was ready for the wedding. I immediately wrote to both the Hungarian embassy in Stockholm and to my aunt in Hungary to see if they could help acquire my birth certificate. But the process dragged on. Gustav and I decided to rent a room in Katrineholm for me to live in when I arrived there in mid-January 1947. The priest had told us that even if I did not get my birth certificate, he could marry us as soon as I

*Agnes, 1947.*

had lived in Sweden for two years. By March 2, 1947, we had all the documentation that was needed, and we were married the same day in a room set aside for marriages in the Malm congregation in Katrineholm. I wore the two-piece dress I'd made in Loka Brunn.

One of Gustav's colleagues, a bartender, and our landlord served as witnesses. The landlord also bought a big cake and made coffee in his little apartment after the wedding ceremony, which took place at 3:00 in the afternoon. Between the hours of 5:00 and 8:00 in the evening, I had to work an extra shift in the cafeteria. ⚍⚍

## *Agnes & Gustav*
**June 1947, Dalarna, Sweden**

As newlyweds, Gustav and I had a wonderful time in the spring of 1947 in Katrineholm. I worked in the cafeteria, and Gustav attended school. When the course was completed in June 1947, we moved to Dalarna to live with Gustav's father, Emanuel. We were expecting our first child. Gustav worked with his father in the woods, and we saved up to buy furniture.

Emanuel lived in only a small cabin. It had a kitchen with a wood stove and a sofa bed with straw mattress. There were also two other small rooms. Emanuel slept in one room, and Gustav and I slept in a sofa bed in the kitchen. The third room was almost empty. I bought food and other essential goods in a country store and cooked the food for us three and made lunch for working days.

In an old laundry room in the village I boiled our dirty clothes in a large container. A full day each week was spent washing Gustav's and Emanuel's dirty work clothes. When it rained, we hung the wash on lines in our kitchen. Gustav brought in water from a stream every night for cooking and hygienic purposes.

One summer morning, I woke up with a red rash that itched. I searched all over and then found bed bugs in the crevices of the sofa bed. We carried the bed outside. I scrubbed it thoroughly and poured boiling water into all the sofa crevices. Then we poured hot lye water over the couch. I found new straw with which we replaced the old in the mattress cover, which also had been thoroughly cleaned. The bugs disappeared, and we slept well on the sofa bed until August, when we moved.

Emanuel and Gustav got jobs at a paper mill that included a two-room worker's apartment. We lived there for only six weeks, until Gustav got an office job in a motor vehicle repair shop. His task was to prepare invoices, calculate the payroll, and manage accounts. We lived in a small room next to the workshop; the room had a hotplate for cooking, and a cold water tap was available outside. The room was drafty, but September 1947 was warm. It was impossible, though, even to consider living there in the winter with a small baby. The district nurse visited, and she told us that if we did not find a better place to live, the baby would be taken from us to live in a nearby orphanage. About October 1, a car salesman knocked on our door. He had learned of our situation from the district nurse. He offered us an apartment upstairs in his home. The apartment was a large room and a kitchen with hot and cold running water; the bathroom was shared with another apartment. Gustav and I moved into it right away, grateful to have a draft-free place for our baby.

The following day, I went into labor, and the day after that our beautiful little Agnes Mari, with long black hair and white skin, was born. She was round, well formed, and weighed eight and a half pounds. The nurses in the maternity ward combed little Agnes's hair and placed a small red bow in it. Then they went around to the other wards and showed her off. I think I was the first foreign woman to give birth in the hospital, and her hair was exceptional. My hair was brown, and Gustav's was blond.

We stayed in the hospital for eight days, as was the custom, and then baby Agnes and I went to stay with a cousin of Gustav's in Hofors. Our time with Joel and Olga was indeed a blessed time. Olga washed the diapers and bathed the baby at night. Our baby girl was kind enough to sleep until morning.

In the winter, Gustav got an office job in a furniture store in Storvik. The store owners also ran a carpenter shop and were undertakers. When Gustav began, their finances were in chaos; no one managed the office. Gustav found large outstanding debts that were owed to the firm and had not been paid, so he began collecting them. Gustav turned the company's loss into a profit.

In the autumn of 1948, when little Agnes (whom we sometimes called Mari) was eleven months old, I started feeling sick, and the doctor said that I was pregnant again. During the spring of 1949, Gustav would take little Agnes for a ride on his bike in the evenings. We had bought a practical child seat that was mounted on the bicycle frame. And even on Sundays, they took a bike ride, so I could cook Sunday dinner in peace.

On July 20, 1949, after the radio's evening news, I began to ache and a half hour later I had a pushing contraction. We immediately went to the hospital. Oskar Håkan was born almost right away. They had barely put me on the birthing table when he was born. ⋙

*Agnes with Mari and Håkan.*

## Agnes & Gustav
**1951, Borlänge, Sweden**

After Gustav had worked a year for a furniture company, he applied for a secretarial position at Stora Kopparberg Vocational School in Borlänge. He got the job and became the headmaster's

*Gustav in his office in Borlänge.*

secretary. We were offered a newly built two-room apartment in a residential area popularly called Grini. I really enjoyed the apartment; it was free of drafts and had hot running water. Finally, I had a refrigerator. ❋

# FINDING THE CHURCH OF JESUS CHRIST, 1952–1960

## *Agnes & Gustav*

**1952–1953, Borlänge, Sweden**

In a basement apartment in our building, the Mission Church had a Sunday School where we let Mari and Håkan go every week. I visited different churches in Borlänge, but none of them really appealed to me. I continued searching.

I discovered that a Hungarian Jewess lived in one of the neighboring apartments. She was married to a Swedish man, and they had two small children. Two American missionaries lived with them. This neighbor lent me a copy of the Book of Mormon, which she said was about a Jewish prophet who was commanded by God to sail across the ocean, together with his family. I was intrigued, and Gustav and I started reading the book. Soon we discovered that the book went hand in hand with the Bible.

When the neighbor and her family left for America, they auctioned off all their belongings. Nonetheless, the missionaries remained another month in the empty apartment and borrowed two cots from us. One month later they returned the cots to us, and I told them that I had read the book. They wanted to discuss the book and their faith with Gustav and me.

Every Sunday for months, the missionaries visited us in our home. The first two missionaries were transferred and new ones came in their place, but our conversations continued. Both Gustav and I felt that the book contained important truths. I understood and recognized it when I read that after His resurrection Jesus Christ appeared to people in the Americas. That made sense because He had told those in Palestine that He had other folds, which He would also visit.

Gustav did as it said in the book to do: he asked God in prayer with a sincere heart whether the book was true, and he got a convincing answer to his prayer. But it took ten months before we were finally baptized into The Church of Jesus Christ of Latter-day Saints.

Our baptism day was quite an experience. The leaders of the Church in Sweden came from Stockholm and took our whole family in a car to Gävle. We were baptized there in a small river

*Agnes and Gustav with Håkan and Mari, 1952.*

outside the city. It felt like being baptized in the Jordan River. A quiet peace prevailed, and I felt a great inner joy. Afterwards, we went to the chapel in Gävle. There we were confirmed, and the children were blessed. Many members were present, and afterwards we drove seventy-five miles back to Borlänge.

In our apartment, we began to have Sunday School for our family, two missionaries, and two or three other members. The adults had discussions in the living room, and I taught the children in the kitchen. One month after our baptism, a neighbor lady named Lilly Blomkvist was baptized; her husband, Ivar, chose not to join the Church. They had two children: Ingvar, six years, and Ingrid, eight years. After that we and Lilly took turns hosting Sunday School. One Sunday we met at Blomkvists' and the next Sunday in our apartment. We found an older woman who belonged to the Church, and along with Lilly Blomkvist and a few other women, we started our weekly Relief Society meetings. After a few months, the Church rented a basement, and we held both Sunday School and Relief Society there. ❖

## Agnes & Gustav
**1954, Borlänge, Sweden**

On a sunny morning, April 15, 1954, our wonderful little girl whom we named Veronika was born.

Gustav was called to be the leader of our Church congregation in the very small but growing branch. For a time, the meetings were held alternately in leisure facilities and members' homes. But in 1954 the Church bought a centrally located villa and

*Mari, Agnes, Veronika, and Håkan, 1954.*

> *When Gustav and Agnes Palm were baptized in 1953 in Borlänge, in the Dalarna area, a branch was organized. It covered an area that stretched some 250 miles from north to south and about 125 miles from east to west. The prewar Church membership records had names of many members living in remote villages around Dalarna who had chosen to stay in Sweden and not emigrate to the United States. Those members, who had been baptized in the years between 1900 and 1939, were visited by Agnes and Gustav during their holiday trips around the Dalarna region in the 1960s.*

turned it into a chapel. Twenty to twenty-five members attended our meetings in the chapel, which held fifty to sixty people sitting in secondhand cinema folding chairs. As branch president, Gustav had a directory of all Church members living in Dalarna. Many had become members at the beginning of the 1900s and had lapsed into inactivity. Many other members had emigrated, and therefore throughout Dalarna there was not a single congregation remaining. The branch in Borlänge was the first since the early 1900s. ⇥⇤

## *Agnes & Gustav*
**1954–1955, Borlänge, Sweden**

We decided to build a home with four rooms and a kitchen. We had not saved much money, but Gustav's company gave four thousand crowns to those who signed up to build their own villa. It was in the form of an interest-free loan that would be written off in ten years. The rest we took as loans from the municipality and the state. Gustav built most of the house himself, even though he was called up for a month for Swedish military refresher training. Our house was the first in the area that was ready for occupancy.

Gustav worked on it every night from 5:00 until 10:00 but never on Sundays. ⇝

## *Agnes & Gustav*
**1957, Borlänge, Sweden**

In our ten-year-old Ford Anglia, we traveled around looking for the people whose names were in the member directory. I remember particularly a trip to a woman who lived in Sälen, about 130 miles from Borlänge. The car's radiator cracked on the road, so we had to refill it with water very often. The house where the woman lived was a dilapidated, two-story, former country store. The woman was in her eighties and lived with her mentally disabled daughter who was in her fifties. A dozen cats lived with them. The mother had joined the Church in 1905

*In their 1947 Ford Anglia, Agnes and Gustar drove round the whole area of Dalarna in the summers to find Church members. Missionaries often accompanied them.*

at Svartensgatan in Stockholm. Despite her isolated existence, she had preserved her faith through the years and was delighted when we knocked on her door. We managed to help her twice a year travel to the chapel in Borlänge.

While we were out finding the old members, "Aunt Elida" was the babysitter at home. Elida was in the Relief Society and had a disability, a bad hip and one leg that was four inches shorter than the other. But that did not stop her from riding her bike every Sunday the two miles from her home to the chapel. She pedaled her bicycle with her walking stick on one pedal and her healthy leg on the other. The only child care payment Elida requested was a large jar of mountain-brewed whey cheese, which she ate directly out of the jar with a teaspoon. ⇒⋅⇐

## *Agnes & Gustav*
**1955–1957, Borlänge, Sweden**

While Gustav was at work, the missionaries asked that I visit a woman who lived in Bullermyren. She had been taught about the Church, and the missionaries wanted me to give her support. The August days were very rainy, windy, and cold, but we had a cover for the baby buggy, and we wore rain gear. Of course I pushed the buggy, and Håkan and Mari walked on each side of it. It took us about an hour to walk the mile and a half to Bullermyren. At our knock, the woman opened the door and said that her husband had forbidden her to let us in. We had no choice but to turn around and return home. Many thoughts went through my head on the way, especially when the children became tired and difficult.

Two weeks later, I met the woman, whose name was Nanny Jakobsson, in the middle of town just outside a store. I asked her if she had stopped studying with the missionaries. She answered that she had decided to be baptized the following week. Her husband had allowed her to do as she pleased. She told me that she had had a bad conscience after she turned me and my children away at the door.

"I thought that if the gospel was so important that you went out into the storm with your three children to visit me, then it must be the truth and love that gave you the power to make that long walk. I prayed and received a strong response. Now," she said, "I hope to become a worthy member."

The very fact that I had walked with the children through the city in the rain to visit her was a stronger message than the spoken one I told her. On the same day that Mari was baptized, Nanny Jakobsson was also baptized. She became a faithful and loving member of the Church and was an inspiring teacher of children and adolescents.

When Veronika was about three years old and Mari and Håkan were ten and eight years old, we learned we were having another child. We hoped that the pregnancy would go well because I had had a miscarriage about a year earlier. On March 25, a wonderful little girl we named Kristina Margareta was born. She was a very pleasant, very cuddly baby with big, beautiful, blue eyes.

We planned to take our first trip to the temple in Zollikofen, Switzerland, in the summer of 1957. We had saved money for the journey. Before the trip, I bought a baby bottle and powdered baby formula, just in case, even though I thought I had plenty of milk myself. In our new, black, four-door Morris Minor, we began the journey from Borlänge on a June evening. Håkan sat next to Gustav in the front seat. The back seat had Mari with Veronika on her lap, and I sat with Kristina lying in a stroller bed. Veronika and Kristina slept all night. Mari and I nodded occasionally. Håkan was awake and alert throughout the night in the front seat. And as usual, he questioned everything he saw.

At dawn, we arrived in Skåne. I was fond of the great plains surrounding it, which reminded me so much of the Hungarian Great Plain. We rested in a grove of trees, took care of Kristina, and then proceeded to Malmö, where we booked into a hostel in the middle of town. There we met more people with whom we would travel by train to Zollikofen. We got a room with five beds. After we were settled, we took a walk in a nearby park, and Gustav went to a briefing about the trip. He arranged it so he could park the car beside the local chapel while we continued our journey.

The children and I went back to the hostel. The children took showers, and we went to bed early. At 6:00 in the morning we got up, ate breakfast, and went down to a waiting bus that took us via a ferry to Copenhagen's main railroad station. We were really disappointed when we were told that the sleeping car for which we had booked tickets would not show up. Our family and the Malm family from Jönköping were the only ones with children.

During the first night we were on the train, it seemed that my milk dried up, and Kristina screamed. I got some hot water from the dining car and mixed the dried powdered milk into it. But when I unscrewed the bottle, the nipple portion broke off and went down into the mixture, which was then full of broken glass. Desperate, I prayed earnestly for help. After only five or ten minutes, a Swedish woman who was on the train told me that she had a baby at home in Sweden who was being fed with the bottle while she was in Switzerland. She was thrilled to breastfeed Kristina. For morning and evening meals, my milk proved to be sufficient, and the Swedish woman, whose name was Birgit Hedberg, provided milk in between.

In the morning, the conductor on the train took pity on us families and showed us to empty first-class compartments. He said that in the absence of sleeper compartments, this was the best he could offer.

In Zollikofen, Switzerland, we were housed in a big room

in the old railway hotel. Our family shared three giant beds with huge puffy feather covers, and Kristina slept in the bedding that came with her pram. In the room were two large sinks with hot and cold water that were good to bathe Kristina in.

I taught Håkan and Mari to say in German, "Warmes Wasser, bitte." With that little vocabulary they could run down to the restaurant with a bottle and come back with the bottle filled with warm water.

*Agnes and Gustav at the temple in Zollikofen, Bern, Switzerland, 1957.*

The highlight of the trip was when our family was sealed for eternity in the temple's sealing room. The children were like little angels when we surrounded the altar.

I will never forget how happy Gustav and I were that the children were close by when we went to sleep that evening. ⚡

## Agnes & Gustav

**Late 1950s and early 1960s, Borlänge, Sweden**

During a meeting in the chapel, I observed a well-built man sitting on the back row. He belonged to another church and was a brother of one of our members. Toward the end of the meeting, without being invited he went straight up to the pulpit and cursed the Church, saying that it was the work of Satan. After this rant, Gustav, who was conducting the meeting, asked if anyone wanted to add something. If not, we would finish in the usual way with a hymn and prayer, which we did.

In the meeting was another visitor who was studying with the missionaries. We thought she would never come back after what had happened. But to our amazement, the event was crucial to her decision to become a member. She said she had never seen such tolerance and restraint as that showed by the Church members. She didn't believe that any other church would have allowed the man to speak as he did without a strong, bitter rebuttal. The woman's name was Ellen Bäck, and she became a good friend of our family. Every Christmas Eve, she was a guest in our home.

On May 15, 1960, when Kristina was three, Per was born. He was a small, sweet, dark boy. The late 1950s and early 1960s were our happiest and busiest years. We spent a lot of time building up our house and putting the garden in order. At the same time, a steadily growing membership in the Church demanded a lot of work. In the late 1950s, the former owner of the chapel moved out of the apartment above the chapel, and Gustav used much of his spare time to repair and rebuild the second floor. We were young, healthy, and happy together—a far cry from the dark days of the war when all had been so unsettled and life held so little happiness or hope. ＝✧＝

# EPILOGUE, 2014

*Håkan Palm*

**Son of Agnes and Gustav**
**2014**

During the process of writing this book, I have gained a renewed understanding of how lasting and deep the effects of my parents' war experiences were, not only on them but also on us five children and even on the lives of their grandchildren. How have we been affected by the things that Mama and Papa experienced during World War II? Which events in my life have in them footprints from the war experiences of my parents, who lived with Papa's hidden war memories and Mama's memories, more open but still protected under a thinly polished surface? The two memories that follow are a small sample of those that have come to mind when I gave free rein to my thoughts, and they give an insight into how Mama and Papa lived with us children.

⋙⋘

Every afternoon, Monday through Friday, at exactly twenty minutes to five, Mama would be in the kitchen preparing supper

Back, left to right: Håkan; Mari and
her husband, Birger Sandum; and Veronika.
Middle: Eva-Linda Sandum, Agnes, and Kristina.
Front: Gustav and Per.

when our daily ritual would begin. During the winter, Mother would turn out the lights in Veronika's room and get a chair. I would stand on one side with my sister Mari on the other and Veronika would be at Mama's knee. At a quarter to five, we could see Papa's bicycle lights about one hundred yards behind the neighborhood electric transformer. We stayed until Papa turned into our housing area and waved to us. He would take his bike down into the basement, and then we would hear him climbing up the stairs to us. Mama would open the door for Papa, and as a four- or five-year-old I saw them kiss each other on the lips. Papa then took off his coat, and we gathered in the kitchen. Every day.

Sometimes Papa would be late. I remember the dark window, the anxious feelings, and how Mama would get up from the chair and hurry into the living room where the black Bakelite phone sat. We would hear her dialing the numbers, and we shared Mama's nervousness while waiting for Papa to answer. The answer did not come—he had (probably) died on the way home!

*The growing branch of the Church in Borlänge, Sweden, 1968.*

Then we would hear Mama dialing our neighbor Greta Borgström. Mama would ask what time it was on her clock, even though our kitchen clock was always correct. For the sake of Mari, Veronika, and me, Mama would attempt to control her jumpiness. That would mean another attempt to sit calmly at the window with us standing next to her. After a delay of between five and seven minutes, Papa's blinking bike lights would inevitably appear one hundred yards behind the transformer. The pieces of our fragile safe world were glued back together.

Without a doubt, Papa learned early in his life the value of being on time. Life with Mama reinforced this attitude to perfection. In adulthood, when my reflections about life and my parents have a different depth, I realize how structuring time was one of Mama's iron bars that kept her silenced anxiety locked up inside. She had lost everything: her home, her friends, her parents, and nearly all her extended family. She was a survivor who had closed off the past and looked ahead. She filled present-day life with family duties and Church service.

Sometimes her earlier life would creep out and then be toned down by Papa: "It'll all work itself out in the end." And we often heard Mama say: "When Per is married, I have done my part." The responsibility for her children was her great motivation to live strong and be healthy. When all of us had grown up, her inner sorrow erupted.

⇒⇐

In the summer of 1989, a few months before the Berlin Wall fell, my wife, Barbro, and I decided that the family's traditional holiday at Keutschacher See in Carinthia in Austria would be extended so we could take a short trip into Hungary. Mother's only surviving relative, cousin Maria, lived in Keszthely. She had not been captured during the war, having managed to avoid the German SS. We felt a strong challenge to look her up and reconnect with the small splinter that was left of my mother's family.

Maria reminded us of Mother. In rudimentary German, Barbro and I could communicate with her. She took us to a nearby restaurant, where she invited us to enjoy a Hungarian dinner. Maria told us that Mama's father had given his prayer book to her before they were deported to the ghetto. She said she would give the antique prayer book to us the following day so we could give it to Mama. In addition, Maria told of a large painting that my grandfather and grandmother had had hanging above their double bed. The motif was, in the Catholic manner, the Blessed Mary with baby Jesus in her arms. Maria had promised Grandfather she would take good care of this painting. Now Maria was wondering if we could take it to Sweden so Mama could get it back after more than fifty years.

Our joy and anticipation was almost euphoric as we contemplated the possibility of taking home to my mother a bridge between before and after the great catastrophe. The prayer book was worn, small enough to fit in the palm of my hand, and gray. The painting measured twenty-five inches by forty-seven inches. The frame was stucco, about five inches wide, and gold plated. We wrapped the painting in corrugated cardboard and shiny brown paper. With thin hemp twine and tape, we made the package manageable.

During the days we transported the painting through Europe in our travel trailer, and every night I carefully placed it on the rear-facing child's seat in the trunk of our Mercedes Kombi. Every morning I repeated the procedure in the opposite direction. I had exultant feelings about the prayer book and the painting. After all, we were going home with a priceless treasure. As far as we knew, the prayer book and the painting were the only mementos from Mama's earlier life.

When we arrived home, we hurried to open the door of the travel trailer to find the prayer book and remove the picture package with its hemp string now a bit dirty.

Hurriedly we knocked on my parents' door and eagerly waited for Mama's reaction. After she opened the package, she said that she remembered how she as a little girl had stood at the foot of her parents' bed and looked up at the painting. That was all. A little disappointed, we went home. Nonetheless, we felt pleased that we had made a valuable therapeutic contribution.

A few days later, I found the painting and its frame sawed into small pieces in my parents' carport. Why, why, why?

Barbro and I sensed a deep psychological drama behind the sawing apart of the picture and its frame. Mama and Papa never gave a fully satisfactory explanation. My interpretation was that Mama could not deal with such an emotional memory in connection with her childhood and youth. Her survival strategy involved locking old recollections inside herself, and only certain memories were allowed to slip out. Those unlocked memories were intended primarily to give us children hope for the future. In the new world she had created there was no room for her parents' painting of Mary and the infant Jesus. Mama had found another country, another faith, and another prayer. Was that why?

⊰⊱

Papa, who was full of integrity, had little or no distance between what he said and did. He was careful with value judgments and allowed us to make our own decisions. Mama's and Papa's experience was also such that they paid no attention to the question of mediocrity or of being average. The subject never came up. With a background of war, death, and earlier feelings of being forsaken, Papa and Mama stood above gossip, whining, and outrage over "trifles." We lived in a family with clear values. Every Monday evening after dinner, Mama and Papa set aside an hour for family home evening. We talked about such things as honesty or to stand up for what we knew was right or how to cope with challenges and difficulties. We experienced a kind of informal "school of life" with them. Many times, my siblings and I thought it was a boring hour. But Papa and Mama were steadfast; they taught us many moral concepts and trained us to live as fair and honest people. We were often told that we should not be aggressive toward others or disparage their values. We were to show respect and tolerance, not condemnation and arrogance.

We never heard anything negative about the Germans. I never thought about that until my sister Veronika said that in 2009 she met a woman whose surviving Jewish grandfather and father continually fed her hatred and bitterness toward the Germans. In her home, one was not allowed to mention the word *German,* never drive German cars, and definitely not go on holiday to Germany. It would have been good had that survivor heard Mama respond to the question of how she had survived the war: "I felt sorry for the German guards. No one could voluntarily and from within himself decide to do what they did. Poor people!"

I never heard my mother complain that the Germans deprived her of much of her life or that the Communists confiscated the property she was entitled to receive in Hungary. One of Mama's explanations of why she survived was that she had been able to tolerate and accept reality as she interpreted it. Either she lived or she died—it was that simple. And there were always others who needed assistance in the camps.

Her strong innocent faith in God and the strength she received from her father's patriarchal blessing on the way to Auschwitz supported her as she lifted herself up. In addition, I believe that her instincts and the ability to quickly understand, along with the courage to accept surprises and quickly draw action-oriented conclusions, helped her see possibilities to work around the routines that were designed to lead to death.

Papa did not reveal to us his war experiences. In the 1990s, he said he did not talk about them for our sake. The victors always write history, and everything that was related to the German war experience was written and told with great condemnation and denunciation. No one speaks of the approximately seventy thousand

Norwegians who were prosecuted and condemned for being German collaborators. Women in Norway who had children with Germans and their children were exposed to cruel persecution. If our neighbors and playmates were to learn that a volunteer soldier in the Waffen-SS lived in Täpp Street 18, Papa believed we would suffer. And he therefore assumed a very low social profile.

Our mother's attitude was always a bit different: "Hitler destroyed his own life, but I will not let him destroy my life."

Humbly and quietly, Papa performed the tasks that were presented to him or which he decided to undertake himself. He never raised his voice and very rarely moralized over the things we did. We knew what was right and wrong, and therefore we often had the answers to our uncertainty. His attitude was, "You know yourself what you should do." An internal dialogue about what decisions my siblings and I should take in specific situations was the result. And since the resolutions to most quandaries were self-evident and easy for Papa and Mama, we children were influenced to follow a similar path.

In accordance with Mama's and Papa's own understanding and their sense of what is right, my parents have made a remarkable journey in their lives after World War II. They provided security and stability for the whole family. Both have been steadfast in practicing what they learned. Father has selflessly served his fellowmen through the callings he received in the Church. Mother has been loyal in supporting her husband and raising her children, teaching them true principles.

I realize how completely worthless Papa felt after the war. He was an exile, poor and abandoned. He had no clothes, no money, and no social support. It hurt me to learn of the miserable conditions under which he lived.

And I think of my mother, who had to leave behind a privileged life but through intelligence, action, and faith overcame the

Holocaust. After the war Agnes was totally alone—and so was Gustav.

The two met and were drawn to
each another. Together they found
security and an ever-increasing love.
Under normal circumstances, it would
have been quite unlikely that they
would even have met, coming as they
did from such dissimilar backgrounds.
Yet they did meet, and they grew together. What a great heritage we, their
children, share.

Taking the profound decision to
put the lid over the past and not talk
about it affects one's whole attitude to

*Agnes and Gustav, 2004.*

life. Why was it so difficult for Papa to share his own opinions?
Why did he refrain from saying what he thought? Why did he
praise us so little, indeed, almost never? Why did we never invite friends home? Was it necessary to continue hiding from the
trauma of war?

The last question was answered in 1995 when President
Thomas S. Monson revealed Papa's story to fifteen hundred people
and said that they both had been preserved through the war. He
testified that we can have faith in the Lord's intervention, as when
Gustav was ordered by an inner voice to jump one step to the right
during his baptism of fire, or when Agnes was able to duck unseen
into another line at the Auschwitz arrival platform. And both escaped death multiple times.

For me it has become clear why President Monson was inspired in 1995 to reveal Papa's life secret to the public. It has given
Papa the opportunity to be more open and thus to better heal his
war wounds. The amazing thing is how my parents' common faith

has given them, over and over, the inspiration and tools to foster their children and keep themselves whole enough to live a normal family life together.

The years since 1995 represent a new era in my father's life. As a sealer in the Stockholm Sweden Temple he has had opportunity to communicate openly and intimately with couples who came to be sealed and have their eternal love confirmed. And Papa became willing to share his and Mama's inspiring story, not as sad lives to be ashamed of or as victimized lives to feel sorry for, but instead two miraculous lives that met, merged, and will eternally progress.

I feel gratitude when I think of Papa and Mama. They are now (2014) in their nineties, and through many years and humble circumstances, they have built up a large, devoted family that now exceeds more than 125 people. What an example of endurance in everyday life! "Overcoming through love" (*Seger genom kärlek*) is the motto that my father and mother chose for their family crest. When we siblings and in-laws asked Papa why almost all of his 125 descendants have chosen to follow in his footsteps, my father replied, after a long silence, "I do not know." In that humble answer there is more wisdom than ignorance.

*Gustav, a temple sealer emeritus, with Sweden Stockholm Temple president Jan Evensen, 2013.*

How can we, with our simple minds and thoughts, explain all the miracles that preserved Mama and Papa through life in extermination camps and battles at the front? How can we explain all the events,

*Gustav (center) with most of his and Agnes's family members. Agnes, bedridden and in a care center, was unable to attend this reunion, 2007.*

both large and small, that brought two very different people with such opposite life experiences together, welded their lives to each other, and enabled them to live through many difficulties and challenges? What a blessing for them to see children, grandchildren, and great-grandchildren grow up to be good people.

We may not be able to explain all these events, but two classical verses remind us, "My thoughts are not your thoughts, neither are your ways my ways, saith the Lord. For as the heavens are higher than the earth, so are my ways higher than your ways, and my thoughts higher than your thoughts" (Isaiah 55:8–9).

We gratefully see the Lord's purpose in the miraculous merging of these two lives: the Jewish woman who had survived the Holocaust and who noticed the "young man—so miserable, so lean, and so pale, almost green in his face, but with very kind eyes" and the former Waffen-SS soldier who caught the attention of the "unfamiliar brunette woman" serving food at Lergöken in Långshyttan. The two found comfort, companionship, and love with each other. Their life is an outstanding example of how people can overcome cultural differences and in the hopelessness of solitude join together to build a wonderful legacy and bless many lives. No matter how lonely and poor you start, endurance and

*The Palm family crest.*

faithfulness to good values brings day by day and small step by small step a victory that is hard to foresee.

"Overcoming through Love," the Palm family motto, beautifully sums up the lives of two remarkable people who overcame great obstacles and through their enduring love now rejoice in their growing family. What an unlikely yet true story! ⇒⇐

# SOURCES CITED IN HISTORICAL NOTES

"Andra Världskriget [Second World War]." In *Nationalencyklopedin*. Malmö: NE Nationalencyklopedia AB, 2004.

Bruchefeld, Stéphane, and Paul A. Levine. . . . *om detta må ni berätta . . . [About this you have to tell]*. Stockholm: Regeringskansliet, 1998.

"Case No. 10, The Belsen Trial, Trial of Josef Kramer and 44 Others, British Military Court, Luneburg, 17th September–17th November, 1945." In *Law-Reports of Trials of War Criminals*, United Nations War Crimes Commission, Volume II, London, HMSO, 1947. Available at http://www.ess.uwe.ac.uk/WCC/belsen6.htm.

Friedländer, Saul. *Tredje Riket Och Judarna, Del I: Förföljelsens år 1933–39*. Stockholm: Natur & Kultur, 1999. Published in English as *Nazi Germany and the Jews: The Years of Persecution, 1933-1939* (New York: HarperCollins, 1997). Cited here as Friedländer 1.

———. *Tredje Riket Och Judarna, Del I: Utrotningens år 1939-45*. Stockholm: Natur & Kultur, 2011. Published in English as *The Years of Extermination: Nazi Germany and the Jews, 1939-1945* (New York: HarperCollins, 2007). Cited here as Friedländer 2.

Tieke, Wilhelm. *Division Nordland i Strid [Division Nordland in Battle]*. Translated from German into Swedish by Lennart Westerberg and Martin Månsson. Stockholm: Svenskt Militärhistoriskt Bibliotek och författarna, 2011. Originally published as *Tragödie um die Treue*.

"Bergen-Belsen." In *Holocaust Encyclopedia*. United States Holocaust Memorial Museum, Washington, D.C. http://www.ushmm.org/wlc/en/article.php?ModuleId=10005224.

# PHOTO CREDITS

British Imperial War Museums (Sgt. Midgley), 84; (Sgt. H. Oaks), 114, 142; (Sgt. Morris), 138, 143

Mats Ekelund, 163, 167

Dove Elbe, 160

German Federal Archive (Ernst Hofman or Bernhard Walter), 50; (Dieck), 66; (unknown photographer), 100

Lynn M. Hansen, 45, 47, 48, 53, 56

Alfons Heiderich, 71

Långshyttans Brukshistoriska Förening, 185, 192

Carl-Johan Malm, 223

Medal-Medaille.com, 125

Norwegian government (photographer unknown), 24

Helena Österlund, x

Gustav and Agnes Palm family, 3, 4, 7, 9, 12, 13, 15, 16, 17, 21, 26, 37, 46, 194, 197, 198, 201, 202, 204, 205, 207, 211, 214

O. Håkan Palm, 20, 36, 176, 215, 221, 222, 224

Tom A. Paulsen, 31

Russian International News Agency (Zelma), 65

Swedish Military Archive, 69, 77, 79, 93, 96, 120